ANTIQUES FOR AMATEURS

By the same author:

MISCARRIAGES OF JUSTICE

THE LOVE LIVES OF CHARLES DICKENS

ANTIQUES FOR AMATEURS

by

C. G. L. Du Cann

FREDERICK MULLER LIMITED
LONDON

First published in Great Britain in 1962 by
Frederick Muller Limited,
Printed and bound by The Camelot Press Ltd.,
London and Southampton

We are grateful to the Radio Times
Hulton Picture Library, Delieb Antiques Ltd.
and the William Gordon Davis Agency for permission
to reproduce their photographs in this book.

CONTENTS

ILLUSTRATIONS

7

PREFACE

THE aim of this book can be clearly and succinctly stated.

It is written for the express purpose of making elementary knowledge about antiques, easily, rapidly and pleasantly assimilable by its readers. The object is to turn ordinary people (who may or may not already be vaguely interested in, or attracted by, antiques) into knowledgeable collectors, able to have confidence in their newly-instructed judgment.

For the purpose of acquiring antiques to advantage in such a way as neither to be misled nor to mislead oneself, some elementary knowledge at the very least is indispensable. If a little knowledge be a dangerous thing, as the proverb declares, ignorance is much worse. Especially when it comes to buying. A little knowledge is essential to the gaining of more; for in time a deep specialised mastery of one's subject may be confidently built upon elementary principles.

Therefore this book aims at giving that foundation of knowledge absolutely necessary to the beginner, yet the book is not only for beginners. Even if the reader is already an antique-lover keen on the hunt for treasures, he will find his knowledge and experience increased and fortified by reading a work such as this. While this book does not profess to be aimed at the *cognoscenti* and lifelong antique-dealers, both may find something to their taste.

Exclusion or Inclusion

Such a book must necessarily and deliberately limit its scope. The world of antiques is vast; its well-defined territories

9

are numerous. Sometimes their boundaries are sharply defined; sometimes they are blurred. For just as a man may be both a father and a son so may a class of articles comprise both the ancient and modern, like the Anglican hymnal "for use in Churches". Thus coins may be as ancient as Mithridates of Persia or even more ancient; or they may be as modern as a Queen Elizabeth the Second newly minted sovereign intended for limited circulation. Numismatics (as the collecting and study of coinage is called) is such a severely specialised field that it requires more than general knowledge. In fact, a whole treatise would be needed to expound it adequately. The same applies to postage-stamps. Philately is also regarded as a specialised field and outside the scope of antiques.

This convention is so well recognised that no one will criticise a book upon antiques for not dealing with such extremely specialised subjects. But this is not the only limitation. When one has subtracted such sharply-differentiated fields as these from the list, the remaining world of antiques is still too large to be manageable in a single volume. Indeed, a mere encyclopaedia of antiques, however concise, will take up several volumes—and even then strike enquirers as being incomplete or inadequate.

Selection therefore is required. Certain leading subjects of course must be included; as for example, old silver, furniture and ceramics. Omission of these is unthinkable. What of minor fields like horse-brasses (excluded here) or glass paperweights (included here)? The devotee of the former may be indifferent to the latter and vice versa.

On what principles has the author's judgment been exercised in regard to the exclusion, or inclusion, of the lesser fields of collecting? His personal likes and prejudices have played no part in his selection. If they had, since he has been something of a specialist in gold snuff-boxes and Fabergé items for years, these items would not have been treated so lightly and incidentally as in this book. His criterion for inclusion has been the chief needs and requirements of a wide field of readership. Thus comparatively few people collect horse-brasses. Those who do, require little or no book-instruction to follow this hobby with success. On the other hand, glass paperweights have a large and increasing following. The treasure-hunter in this field needs definite knowledge and guidance to safeguard himself from wasting good money on inferior modern specimens.

It is impossible, of course, to please everybody. For example, devotees of Victorian samplers, lovers of old lace or fine Japanese prints may regret their exclusion. But they will probably agree, even if with regret, that some such omissions are inevitable.

Historical and Technical

Having decided what subjects should be treated here, the author had next to decide upon the kind of treatment to be given to the chosen subjects.

When I first began to collect I suffered greatly from the books so eagerly consulted. There were plenty of authoritative treatises of the soundest character by acknowledged, learned experts in their chosen subjects. What did I find in those books? Undisputed scholarship in the utmost detail: historical research and the technicalities of manufacture; pedantic completeness to such a degree as to foil the most captious fellow-specialist or critic amongst the connoisseurs.

11

To the ordinary reader the tomes were unreadable and unrewarding, the weight of learning being wearisome in the extreme. Excellent for the esoteric few, such books give all the ordinary person does not require and nothing that he does. From such volumes the reader asks for bread and he receives a stone. The stone may be a precious one, but who can live upon such a diet as diamonds.

If you forswear such exhaustive (and exhausting) literature, as I confess I did, you find yourself taking refuge in books upon antiques of the cosy, chatty order, usually written by feminine egoists who are also sentimentalists. Gush is no substitute for the practical, down-to-earth information that the antique-hunter needs if he is to pursue his hobby with pleasure and profit.

These two types of book ought to be excommunicated. They are already cursed by serious antique-followers who long for a plain, straightforward work which they can use as "a guide, philosopher and friend". Here I hope is one: at any rate, I have done my best to make it so.

No doubt the books I criticise can be justified. Specialists writing for specialists are entitled to state everything possible on their subject. Enthusiasts writing for their fellow-enthusiasts may wax sentimental and engage in chit-chat. But to everyday collectors urgently needing practical guidance on how to collect to advantage both types of book are a bore and a waste of time!

Indeed, such books do the last thing they desire to do: discourage the beginner who needs encouragement. The technicalities of primitive glass-blowing in medieval days or the detailed story of an individual ceramics-factory, or the story of Hungarian silver's heyday in the time of King Matthias Corvinus in the twelfth century, may interest the serious student. Such matters merely befog the practical collector. He is in quest of useful guidance in his daily pursuit of acquiring desirable, and desired, antique pieces.

Some knowledge of history and technicalities is needed by him, of course. But anything beyond the indispensable is a positive hindrance to the reader seeking practical help in his task.

The Wrong—and the Right—Approach

Too many books upon antiques are utterly old-fashioned, not in their substance but in their approach. Our everyday world is a modern and not an antique environment. It is in *this* modern setting that collected antiques have to live and flourish. Our homes are not museums.

Modern home-conditions cannot be ignored in collecting. Restricted living-room in modern flats and small houses—as dealers know only too well, if authors do not—have to be taken into account. "The Way We Live Now" has to be considered in regard to antiques, as with anything else. These factors and similar ones strongly influence the trend of modern collecting. Tea-urns and large Chippendale book-cases—however fine in themselves—today are not sought by the average collector. Therefore detailed expatiation upon such objects is wasted upon him.

The rich man in his castle may collect the tea-urns and book-cases in quantity, if he will: he has room for them. The poorer man in his cottage (or suburban villa) has little. Therefore such objects have been excluded from this book.

Other exclusions are on similar lines. In a book for average English collectors it is absurd to dilate upon Italian Renaissance furniture: its grandiose magnificence and splendour suit only the sumptuous salons of ducal palaces. Nor is it of use to deal at length with the glories of Louis

XIV, XV or XVI cabinet-making. The same is true of early Sévres, Dresden, Meissen and other continental porcelain. None of these topics therefore, is treated in this book, fascinating though such subjects are to advanced collectors.

The High Price Bogey

Surely, too, it is of little use and perhaps only disheartening to give lengthy accounts of the astronomical prices fetched by exceptionally rare pieces at such fashionable auction-rooms as Christie's or Sotheby's at the moment. Such prices are not for the average collector. In any case the more serious daily newspapers such as *The Times*, *Telegraph* or *Guardian* can be up-to-the-minute with such information. In times of money-devaluation, auction, and even shop, prices rapidly become out of date.

Indeed, high prices scare off many a prospective collector. Unfortunately, a general belief exists that antiques are highly fashionable and therefore extremely dear. The average person does not realise that a lot of good antique furniture even today is cheaper, better designed and better made than its modern counterpart. "High prices" are sensational news. There is no news-story in reasonable, or below-ordinary, prices. Accordingly they go unchronicled.

What with supposedly outrageous prices, over-emphasis upon fakes and forgeries, and vague identification-data, is it any wonder that many people, attracted though they may be, are scared to become collectors?

"No use" they say despondently. They believe that genuine antiques cost the earth because high prices hit the newspaper-headlines. They believe that the antique-dealers are cheats on the strength of tales of how one of them

14

bought an apparently dirty old daub in a tarnished gold frame from poverty-stricken old-age pensioner Mrs. Jones, and sold this Old Master (for such it later proved to be) at Sotheby's to an American millionaire. They also say that all the real treasures have been snapped up long ago, so it is too late for any amateur to start collecting. The attitude of even the educated portion of the English public about antique-collecting is generally defeatist.

If you doubt this, talk to non-collectors. People will "have a flutter" on almost anything but an antique. Towards antiques and antique-dealers their attitude is one of mistrust. (Not that antiques ought to be taken merely on trust or any such purchase be merely speculative. It can and should be a certainty, or a near-certainty.)

A Book For Mr. and Mrs. Everyman

It is to be hoped that this book may do something to dissipate this general distrust. Most antique-dealers are friendly, courteous and helpful, as ready to teach, as to learn from, their customers. Very few dealers are ignoramuses or greedy cheats seeking to palm off forgeries and fakes upon the unsuspecting purchaser.

So what, in fact, do would-be collectors want from such a book as this? If they are reasonable, sensible people like Mr. and Mrs. Everyman, next to money they want help, heartening guidance and encouragement in the practical task of deciding what to acquire and what to refrain from buying. This book tries to fulfil these needs. But it does not pretend that book-knowledge is enough. It preaches the sound doctrine that the collector must use his own eyes and fingers upon any article presented to him. A book may teach him much, yet he can and must teach himself more

15

in auction-rooms, shops and museums. Theoretical knowledge is not enough unless backed by practical personal experience. Together they should lead to successful understanding of how to collect antiques.

So read this book—and then, good hunting!

1

Making a Good Beginning

WHAT are antiques?

To some people this may sound as foolish as the question asked by the newspaper-proprietor Edward Hulton the First. Told by one of his editors of the intention to print Keats, Hulton enquired suspiciously: "What are Keats?"

Nearly everyone has a vague idea that antiques are things that are old. But what sort of things? And how old?

It is necessary to be more precise. "Any old thing" is not an antique within the special, accepted meaning of that term. An antiquated appearance is no guide. Something more is required. A mere hunk of wood, roughly hewn, however ancient, would not be classed as "an antique".

A good working definition is a relic of the past which enjoys general esteem, and therefore value, in the present. The key-words are "esteem" and "value". That expression "a relic of the past" again is not precise enough. Something made only yesterday or last week is decidedly not an antique.

Very well then! We must define some period of the past. The usual date taken is 100 years ago, so amend our working-definition accordingly. There is nothing sacrosanct about the 100-year period, but the United States law once allowed antiques of that age and over to be imported free of duty. So it is a convenient yardstick of time, generally accepted in the antique world.

"An antique is a relic of the past, 100 years old or more, that enjoys general esteem and therefore value at the

present day." This is a useful practical definition and will
suffice as a general guide to the subject.

"Relics of the past having value" covers a very wide
field of human possessions. You recall how firmly that
Charles Dickens' character, Mr. Wemmick, pinned his
faith to portable property? He was perfectly right, but
would have been even more so if his movables were antiques.

The field is enormous, so let us glance at some of the
classes under the heading of antiques:

Furniture; glass, ceramics (porcelain and pottery); enamels; pewter; gold and silver; jewellery; clocks and watches;
arms and armour; books and book-bindings; needlework,
including lace; tapestries, carpets and rugs; miniatures; pictures (oil-paintings and water-colours); drawings and prints;
oriental netsuké and inro; Toby jugs; Wedgwood and other
ware; musical-boxes; *chinoiserie*; coins, medals and tokens;
stamps; bronzes; silhouettes, wax and glass pictures; dolls
and dolls' houses; Chinese jade and nephrite; paperweights;
pharmacy jars; wine, spirit and sauce labels; wall-mirrors;
statuary; candelabra and lustres; papiermâché; maps and
globes; ivories; Russian ikons; autographs; horse-brasses;
articles of vertu (including vinaigrettes, snuff-, comfit- and
patch-boxes, etc.); walking-sticks; fans; tea-chests and tea-
caddies; terra-cottas and *pietre dure*.

All these classes are "well worthy of the connoisseur's
attention and the collector's acquisition". Long as the list
is, it is by no means exhaustive.

Although all these classes are regularly bought as antiques, some of them are so specialised that the ordinary
antique-dealer keeps none, or only a few in his shop. For
example, coins, postage-stamps and pictures are regarded
as requiring such deeply specialised knowledge that dealers
confine themselves to one only of these, and very often
to nothing else. Again you may pick up a modern book

entitled *Antiques* by a well-known general dealer and find it confines itself almost entirely to furniture and ceramics. Few antique-dealers or collectors will recognise old books as antiquities, however ancient they may be. Quite justifiably dealers expect to find them only in booksellers' shops and at book-auctions.

However, the beginner wandering around the shops where antiques and pseudo-antiques are to be found, very quickly picks up a knowledge of where he may expect to find what interests him.

People, of course, will collect and hoard anything: flimsy discarded match-boxes, old clothes, out-of-date newspapers, rubbish of every sort and kind; in a word, junk, virtually of no value at all. There is all the difference in the world between hoarding rubbish and collecting antiques which carry esteem and value with them. The first is folly; the latter good sense. One brings futility and annoyance in its train; the other, solid satisfaction, pleasure and profit.

Yet however different, senseless hoarding and the sensible collecting of antiques, may, if you are not careful, overlap. Genuine antique specimens may be down-graded to virtual rubbish by irreparable damage of some kind or by excessive wear and tear.

Take a fine wine-decanter of George the Third's time: undoubtedly that is a genuine antique. However, if its glass stopper is missing, a bit of its lip broken away and the body of the decanter cracked, only a foolish person would buy it. One of the earliest lessons the beginner should learn is that in any field where perfect specimens exist, these should be obtained. The best in its kind is good enough for us all. In being warned against the purchase of rubbish, do not be misled into avoiding junk-shops altogether. Amongst the rubbish, real treasure may be found by the discerning and at bargain-prices, too.

The list of articles which properly comprise antiques gives you very little idea of the vastness and variety that lie concealed. (And remember that you have already been told explicitly that the list is far from exhaustive.)

Let me illustrate by taking the category of "oil-paintings" alone. A moment's thought will remind you of the highly distinct and specialised classes in this category. The most ignorant of us know the general look of "Old Masters", and the wide differences between the Dutch, Spanish, English, French and Italian schools, and realise how widely different a Spanish Goya is from a French Gauguin, an Italian Raphael or Canaletto. Even the most passionate, enthusiastic and leisured of collectors can hardly hope to master the whole field of antiques, or be equally knowledge-able about a number of different kinds of antique.

It is essential to specialise. You will almost certainly find that is what you desire. Not every class of antique will appeal equally. Some indeed will not appeal to you at all; rather may they repel you. I cannot imagine myself collecting horse-brasses or general Victoriana and though I would always find pleasure in looking at a Charles Condor fan, a collection of fans would seem to me a trivial and trifling occupation. I regard them as a waste of life-time and hard-earned cash. Others may feel quite differently about fans. I can well understand and do applaud such collectors but I think myself no whit superior for preferring gold and silver vinaigrettes, snuff-boxes and the like.

It is all a question of taste and idiosyncrasy. You must follow your own taste and interest if you are to be a suc-cessful collector of antiques. Your taste will refine itself and your interest will increase with time.

Undoubtedly you will have heard that antiques are money-makers: a sensible and laudable hope is that you may add to your income by collecting. In these days of inflation, experience shows that prices are ever on the rise. By knowledge, prudence and foresight, the amateur—even the beginner—very often *can* make money in this field without much difficulty.

If you are tempted by the desire to make money, do not say to yourself: "Let me choose for my field the branch in which the quick money can be made, irrespective of where my taste and interest lie." That is not the way to do it. It is as foolish as if you said, "Diamonds are more valuable than anything else; therefore I will trade in them alone, although I have not the slightest *flair* or interest for them and cannot tell the difference between a white sapphire and a brilliant." It is better, you will agree, to make a fortune out of rubbish than go bankrupt over diamonds. The same rule applies to antiques.

The only way for the amateur to make a profit, as well as to have pleasure out of antiques, is to follow personal interest and taste. Only then will you attain the "*flair*" which is everything in advantageous antique-collecting.

So—choose your field—or fields but not too many, especially at first. Choose what interests and appeals to you. Even the ordinary provincial antique-dealer who, of necessity, must collect a variegated, miscellaneous stock, has some items to which he is personally indifferent, and trades much better in those he really knows, loves and understands. The rule for the amateur is the same as for the professional.

Having chosen your field, do not rush madly into making purchases. You have a lot to learn yet: about fine specimens, prices, and learning to recognise the great gulf between the buying-price and the selling one. Go and look at many specimens of the thing (or things) in which you are interested, in a variety of shops, museums and auction-rooms. Soon—but not too soon—you will be able to show discernment.

In choosing specimens adhere rigidly to these rules. Ask yourself three questions: (1) Is it beautiful? (2) Is it rare? (3) Is it valuable? You must, of course, relate these questions to its kind. Beautiful, rare and valuable specimens are what you should aim at acquiring.

Give a proper interpretation to these key-words. Beauty includes perfection in the sense of being unworn and undamaged (if that may be): in "mint" or *fleur de coin* condition, as collectors often say. Value may be based upon more considerations than beauty or rarity. A silver piece by Paul de Lamerie or Paul Storr or Hester Bateman may have value because of its maker. A book I possess has acquired increased value because it was successively the property of William Wordsworth and Thomas Hardy, both of whom wrote their names upon the fly-leaf. But for these associations the book would have no value at all. As it is, it is of great value and immediately saleable. It was given to Hardy by his friend Sir Sydney Cockerell. When he was 93 years old I showed it to him and he told me how greatly Hardy had valued it.

Up to this point I have advised my reader as though he intended to make some kind of a collection. It may be that you feel tempted to acquire just a few antiques merely for personal use and pleasure. Is that worth while, you may ask?

The answer emphatically is: "Yes—from every point of view." As stated in the Preface, antiques—especially furniture—compare very favourably with modern furniture in craftsmanship, beauty and even in price. Modern furniture depreciates in value as second-hand directly you acquire it. Fine antique furniture tends to rise, and over the years to go on rising in value. Though it has stood the wear of generations already, it will outlast modern stuff because its workmanship is more conscientious and skilled, and the materials used are better.

However, antique furniture may be costly. You fear that specimens are rarely picked up at bargain-prices so you say: "Will not fine modern 'reproductions' of the antique, made by reputable firms, be equally good and a lot cheaper?"

Fine reproductions are not entirely to be despised, but they are never equal to the originals. Nor can they give the pride and satisfaction that the possession of an original gives to its fortunate owner. As to cost: provided you do not pay an altogether extravagant price, the best is cheapest in the long run. Nor should you overlook the fact that an antique will generally outlast both you and your heirs.

From the viewpoint of utility, of course, certain modern furnishings are superior to the antique. Who would prefer a Georgian warming-pan for the bed to the latest safe type of electric-blanket?

After reading this chapter you are probably ready to begin, since now you know how to begin. Let me give you this final warning. Useful as this and other books may be as a source of inspiration and information, no literary help can replace the use of your own eyes, ears and head. Personal acquaintance with antiques should go hand-in-hand with book acquaintance.

2

The Pleasures and Profits

To strengthen your desire to make a good beginning, as laid down in the first chapter, it is relevant to consider what pleasures and profits are to be expected from this pursuit and how best they may be attained. They can be substantial—far more so than in most amateurs' hobbies.

Hunting of any kind is a pleasure, and treasure-hunting no exception. The hope of success rises to a climax in success itself, sometimes after a long search to obtain a particularly desired article at the right reasonable price. Nor is this all. Possession of an antique is a joy in itself; it can please both the eye and the mind. There is satisfaction too in the reflection that neither one's time nor one's money has been wasted but, in fact, has been expended to advantage.

There is the admiration—it may even be envy—which this possession arouses in your friends and acquaintances. It is a harmless, innocent pleasure to take pride in your acquisitions and to show them to your friends.

To appreciate these joys to the full, it is necessary to experience them. Conscious knowledge enables you to do this for attainment and realisation afford a deep satisfaction in themselves.

It is not necessary to enlarge further upon the pleasures of collecting antiques. The beginner soon realises them for himself. In any case, the enthusiasm of collectors is notorious.

But—do antiques pay? In general, the answer is, yes, even nowadays, when they cost apparently too high prices. This may be a temporary phenomenon due to inflation and the continued devaluation of money at the present day. Most emphatically it ought not to be counted upon to last. It may, but it is wiser to act upon the idea that it may not. The right view is that only by careful, prudent, knowledgeable purchase, can antiques make profits—and handsome ones at that.

Perhaps you are not out for financial gain. Even so, you still may wish to avoid loss. For my part, I advocate that from the very beginning the amateur should aim at a profit. This has many more advantages besides the obvious one. Profits are good in themselves. The pursuit makes certain that the antique-collector will be a keener observer and selector of what is really worth while and take precautions against being cheated by others, or deceived by fakes.

"It must be difficult to learn what is a fake and what is genuine. And how to be a judge of the real thing." Not at all! One learns to collect safely—by collecting! Nothing is easier and more pleasant to learn. Hints will be given by me on how to detect fakes and forgeries under the respective classes of antiques. Meanwhile, how good it is both for body and mind to wander in town and country, searching for things rare and beautiful with which to adorn one's home or add to one's possession. There are few more innocent, pleasurable and profitable occupations. Today you can still buy fine old china by searching for bargains for less than you can buy fine new china. Antique furniture of quite good quality, especially picked up a piece at a time, will cost you less than furniture new, durable and as fine-looking. And the old things are pleasanter to live with and more admired by visitors.

By observation and experience you will soon learn to

discount the general idea that antiques are fabulously dear. Without a doubt some are. Despite high prices tending to go even higher, bargains abound. Only you have to search harder for them.

The time to begin is *now*. Collecting is on the increase. It is no longer confined to the wealthy, leisured classes. Motoring enables the amateur to scout for the treasure he seeks. And the level of good taste is rising fast. Working-men and women are avid collectors nowadays and show great discrimination in their purchases and sound selective judgment.

Non-collectors assume that amateurs are just foolish hoarders. No hobby is more sane and business-like, when properly conducted. Wise collecting means good investing, whether for a speedy or long-term sale.

It is as well to collect freely. Consider what may happen at your death. If the curios and antiques are few, they will be lumped together and sold by the local auctioneer as a "lot". Locals, ignorant of their real value, artistically and commercially, will re-sell in local shops for double the price. That is how bargains go begging in small shops.

On the other hand, if you have a sizeable collection, it will be sent up to Christie's or Sotheby's or somewhere similar. Then it will be auctioned, amongst the knowledgeable, at its true value.

Here are a few cautions for the amateur beginner:

1. Avoid collecting a class of antiques just because it has suddenly become fashionable. There was a craze for old pewter; people paid inflated prices for rubbishy specimens, but the craze died and poor specimens now fetch little.

Again there was a craze for first editions. During that period a friend of mine sold a faded-backed green volume of Bernard Shaw's plays for £25. Like the woman in the parable she "rejoiced and was exceeding glad" having paid only a few shillings for the volume. Today it would not fetch a £5 note. The First Edition Club of the late A. J. A. Symons is dead, and most modern "firsts" fetch relatively little today.

There are fashions in collecting, just as in clothes. And there are fluctuations in prices too, but the rare and beautiful remain valuable.

2. Do not try to collect any class of curio because it is excessively old or excessively rare. Leave that sort of thing to learned men or millionaires. *Sung* porcelain is not for most collectors.

3. Neither should one try to collect what is too common. Late willow-pattern earthenware, for example, is really not worth while. There is too much of it about, and even the early variety tends to suffer in price.

4. Avoid collecting mammoth articles which are bound to prove an unmitigated nuisance. Vast pictures in great gilt frames, cumbersome furniture, thick heavy Bibles and other volumes—all are a mistake. That sort of collecting takes up too much room and is difficult to move. Also it is out of fashion. The likelihood of it returning to favour is small.

5. Finally, never collect what you do not like on its own account. It will almost certainly revenge itself upon you. There is no profit or pleasure in this, because what you dislike you cannot judge without prejudice.

Having been told what *not* to collect you will naturally ask:

"What *shall* I collect for my profit and pleasure?"

This is a question you must answer for yourself. Personally I chiefly collected gold and silver articles, but have other miscellaneous collections. You may not care for gold, silver or metal in general. You may prefer the delicacy of fine china or glass. Or any other of the hundred-and-one things people do collect with avidity! I suggest that at first you need not confine yourself only to one line.

Perhaps it is difficult to pitch on "your own line" straight away. I did not begin by saying: "Only gold and silver for me." I began by being enthralled by the beauty of a small George the Third silver vinaigrette box (which would do admirably as a tablet-container or fit nicely into a waistcoat-pocket). I examined it closely and found it perfect in every way. It cost me eleven shillings, and I bought it at Bath. A year or two later—I had risen to a gold Georgian vinaigrette by then—I sold it without any difficulty for thirty-three shillings to a London shop. I had not simply doubled my money, but trebled it. With prudence and a little luck you may do still better.

Gold and silver work, which can be very high art indeed, appealed to me. Whilst looking at and admiring such articles, amongst many others, I found my chief line. You, too, must do this by experiment.

Before you recognise your line and even after you have done so, it is quite a good idea to collect a class of antique that people are *not* seeking. If in itself the thing is good, beautiful and useful, be assured it will come back into fashion. Indeed, it may soon be the rage. For a time Victoriana of all kinds was despised. Look at the prices it now fetches. For instance, Victorian silver is specially priced as such and its price continually rising.

Remember that beauty and style invariably mean value in the end. The picture of a lovely young girl will always be worth more than that of any man by the same artist. Remember also that rarity is perhaps the chief factor in value.

When you begin, do not be over-enthusiastic and spend more than you can afford. You are in collecting for what you get out of it, not for what the dealers get out of you. Never forget that.

THE PLEASURES AND PROFITS

Go about. Look into shops, museums and auction-rooms. Talk to dealers and curators. Ask questions freely. Be in no hurry to buy. Never grudge a little time spent in study. The museum is an excellent school and there are many books and newspaper articles worth reading at home.

If you live in London, you, as a collector, are especially fortunate. The collections at South Kensington are unparalleled; so is the famous Wallace Collection at Hertford House. The British Museum is also full of treasures.

Generally the museums publish useful handbooks and catalogues. Buy them. Then go round the collections, case by case. You will be astonished at the practical knowledge you will pick up and with what ease you acquire it. A shilling, or an hour, spent in such studies may mean pounds gained in the future.

Above all, do not be depressed by lack of knowledge. The greatest living connoisseur learns something fresh every day. The subject of antiques is almost inexhaustible. That need not make you feel exhausted. Most successful collectors began, as I did, by knowing nothing at all.

3

"Picking Up Gold and Silver"

"I'M on Tom Tiddler's ground, picking up gold and silver."
That triumphant cry is part of an ancient nursery-rhyme of
unknown origin. To the collector it is a very good idea.
One should "pick up" gold and silver, those traditional
treasures of mankind.

Do not shy away from high prices or the idea that antiques of gold and silver are so valuable as to be for the
rich alone. It is true that in themselves gold and platinum
are costly metals. Silver today is so widespread as to be
almost only a semi-precious metal—though in some cases
antique silver may be astronomically high in price, as the
auction-records tell us.

The ordinary person thinks that his wife's or daughter's
rings, bracelets, wrist-watches and the like are possessions
enough, together with—perhaps—his own wrist-watch, studs
and cuff-links and cigarette-case of modern make. To find
these male appendages in gold in the England of today is
rare. Very probably quite well-off families may not have
any antique, and very few modern, gold articles.

It is high time to change these ideas.

A gold box, to take one example (even a tiny vinaigrette
or patch-box of Georgian or Victorian days), is not over-
expensive. I have some small Georgian gold boxes that cost
me in the neighbourhood of £4 10s. each. Today I would
sell none of them below £50. So you perceive that gold
boxes can be quite a good investment over the years.

Indeed, those delicately fashioned boxes in gold or silver called vinaigrettes are well worth attention, especially by the beginner of limited means, paradoxically enough.

Even the possession of a single fine specimen pays one. From the utilitarian standpoint it may be put to constant practical use. It can be used for postage-stamps, aspirin, sleeping-tablets or pills. It can be carried in the male waistcoat-pocket or the feminine handbag with equal convenience. It is pleasant to handle and to look at, or to show to one's admiring friends. Also it makes a pretty ornament, negligently put either on a side-table or on a mantelpiece.

What is a vinaigrette? It is a small box with an interior grid (often beautifully designed and chased) below which is a cavity for a tiny sponge soaked in aromatic vinegar. It was used by our ancestors to keep off prevalent bad smells and to give a pleasant nasal stimulant. Often it was known as "a sponge-box". It was made in all kinds of materials besides gold or silver.

Vinaigrettes, as such, are of comparatively modern origin, ranging in date between the times of King George the Third and Queen Victoria. They derive from the pomander (*pomme d'ambre*) which was much used as a protection from the plague, from fevers and odious smells. This pomander came from the orange. Cardinal Wolsey habitually carried one in his hand: "whereof the meat was extracted and the rind filled up with a sponge wherein was Vinegar and other Confections against the Pestilent Airs. To the which, he most commonly smelt when he was pestered with many suitors."

The beginner who decides to collect vinaigrettes is amply safeguarded. Fakes are almost unknown. The stamps on the gold or silver—such hall-marks as the maker's mark (and others to be detailed later on in this chapter)—keep him straight.

Moreover, as antiques go, vinaigrettes—except the most elaborate and finest gold ones—are cheap. Nor do they tend to fluctuate in price to the confusion of the buyer. Especially in these days, they are inclined to increase in value. The American market buys them, which helps.

For these reasons vinaigrette-collecting is a good, safe introduction to more valuable and important pieces. It provides the indispensable elementary knowledge. Most collectors of gold and silver begin with the little vinaigrette, or its near relatives in size, the patch-box or the spice-box.

Though fakes in vinaigrettes are rare, faulty specimens, those which are damaged, badly worn, mended or defective in mark, are common. Refuse them. Do not be persuaded. If apparently cheap, they are almost always over-priced. Foolish investments, they give no aesthetic satisfaction to their owner in future days when his taste has improved, as it is bound to do with experience.

Gold vinaigrettes, especially, can be obtained in faultless condition. Such specimens, beautiful without and within, with plain clear hall-marks and a finely pierced grid, beautifully designed, are the ones to acquire. Have nothing to do with any but these. If the original sponge and the little leather-covered case are available, so much the better, but these two often-cherished trifles do not really matter.

One especially esteemed form of vinaigrette, usually either in silver or silver gilt, has a raised replica on the outer lid of a famous building, such as Westminster Abbey, the House of Commons, or Byron's home at Newstead Abbey. Most are the work of Nathaniel Mills or another old Birmingham silversmith whose initials can be seen inside the box.

Vinaigrettes are usually rectangular in shape, though numerous other shapes are readily found. The hand-engraving outside and the grid-design inside are very varied

Right, a William and Mary chair. *Bottom left*, a mahogany Gothic armchair; *right*, a chair by Hepplewhite

Left, a chair by Sheraton.
Bottom, two examples of
Chippendale's work

and often perfectly lovely. Vinaigrettes and other small boxes were made both in England and on the Continent, but the English varieties are the greater esteemed. They tend to be more solidly made than the French, which are sometimes thin and flimsy.

Vinaigrettes also exist in pinchbeck. Gold vinaigrettes are generally of 18-carat gold and becoming very rare in the shops. At the time of writing, in England you may have to pay between £25 and £80 for a gold Georgian one, and £20 upwards for a gold Victorian. You will not find many to choose from even in London's Bond Street or in the Rue de la Paix in Paris, for they are quickly and eagerly snapped up.

On the other hand silver vinaigrettes—especially worn condition ones—are quite common. Those of good quality and in a good state of preservation today range between £4 and £6 for Victorian and £6 and £15 for Georgian, in the West End shops. In the smaller London shops or in the provinces you may do better than those prices.

Contemporary with vinaigrettes were spice-boxes holding nutmeg for grating into wine or negus. These were hardly ever of gold but often of silver. I have only seen one gold Georgian nutmeg-grater box. These boxes tend to be cheaper in price than vinaigrettes and are rarely as beautiful. Little patch-boxes (to hold the patches of court-plaster with which gallants and dames ornamented their faces) may be of gold or silver. There are also comfit-boxes, known as *bonnonnières*, well worth acquiring and useful now for other purposes.

After a vinaigrette or other small container, you may wish to go further and buy a fine antique 18-carat gold snuff-box. If you do, nowadays you must go into three figures for an English specimen. Take care to buy an unworn, undamaged and well-marked one; a box in what collectors call "mint condition". Gold boxes usually are in good preservation, for they were taken great care of and, if used, then with great care. Up to the year 1798 English law insisted that gold must be 22-carat. Since then 18-carat gold has been used for the best articles and it is denoted by a crown followed by "18".

The finest gold boxes of all are the French Louis Quinze or Louis Seize gold, or enamel and gold, boxes which reach the summit of the goldsmith's art. These may run you into four figures easily enough and are for millionaires, rather than amateurs. They are exquisite. A visit to the Louvre in Paris is worth while merely to enjoy the sight of the collections of them there. The leading trade-specialists in them in London are Phillips of Bond Street and Wartski of Regent Street and to see their boxes is a liberal education.

Before you buy anything in gold, whether old or modern, you should learn one elementary fact which ordinary well-educated English people rarely do: that the dealer's constant shop-window label "Solid Gold" is a misnomer. It almost invariably denotes 9-carat gold, which, strictly speaking, is hardly gold at all. It means that out of 25 parts of the metal only 9 are gold, the rest being some alloy.

Always see what carat the gold you buy is. As the object, if English, is plainly stamped with the crown and its carat-number, this is easy enough. Further, the metal can be easily tested with a liquid called "aqua regia", a compound of acids. Any jeweller will test your gold for you in two or three minutes and tell you the carat.

In general you should buy only articles of 18-carat gold, which genuinely can be described as gold. However, you need not reject a fine article of 14 or 15 carat gold. Many fine continental antique pieces, notably Russian, are of this lower standard. For example, the great Russian goldsmith and jeweller Carl Fabergé, whose *objets d'art* have remained fashionable—and outrageously expensive—for many years often worked in gold of lower carat than 18. He made marvellous Easter eggs for the Czar. His clocks, cigarette-cases, bell-pushes, umbrella and cane handles, and other pieces, such as his animals carved in semi-precious stones, are eagerly collected—by monarchs and by others who can afford them!

Fabergé pieces are worth your serious attention—even if you cannot afford to collect them. . . .

Turning now from gold to antique silver, the latter is a much more complicated subject. Gold has always been too costly and precious for making up into anything but small articles, chiefly of jewellery for personal adornment. Silver has been employed for an infinite variety of household and other goods.

The first thing you have to learn about silver (and in general this applies to gold also) is that English, Scottish

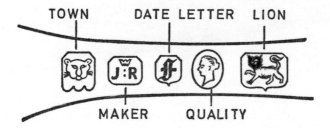

TOWN   DATE LETTER   LION

MAKER   QUALITY

and Irish silver articles are hall-marked in detail for your safety. Nearly everybody knows that British silver has a lion on it. This lion, standing up with paw raised and head facing you, is known as a "lion passant". Few people, other than collectors, trouble about the other marks, though these are of great importance. There may be four, or even six, marks on any piece of antique British silver. As already noticed, first there is the distinctive lion denoting that the metal is silver.

Next, there are the maker's initials. If you possess (as you should) that bible of collectors of gold and silver, Sir Charles Jackson's *English Goldsmiths and Silversmiths Marks*, you will be able to identify the maker of any antique piece by name. Next there is an assay mark (as it is called) denoting the town in England, Scotland or Ireland where the silver was made. A leopard's head denotes London, an anchor Birmingham, Dublin has the harp of Erin crowned, Edinburgh generally the Scottish thistle, Sheffield a crown, and so on. You can find these town-indications in Jackson, Chaffers, and jewellers' pocket-guide and similar books.

Finally, there is what is called the "date" letter. This letter and the shield on which it rests, read in conjunction with the town-mark, enable you to say with positive certainty: "This piece was made in the year ——."

Unless erased by wear and tear these four marks are pretty certainly on almost every piece of British silver you can possibly find. There may be two others, but these are confined to certain periods. They are (1) a figure of Britannia (which began about 1697 in the reign of William and Mary and compulsorily ended in 1718, though you will still find it voluntarily used much later than that). It is put on to indicate the good quality of the silver. (2) The head of the reigning King or Queen from the year 1784 to 1890.

You perceive now that from these marks you can "read" a piece of English silver, antique or modern, as surely and certainly as you can a book. This is a great safeguard to collectors. You do not have to carry the necessary knowledge in your head or even this book of mine about with you.

From any first-class antique jeweller you can obtain a pocket-guide called *Collectors Guide to Marks of Origin on*

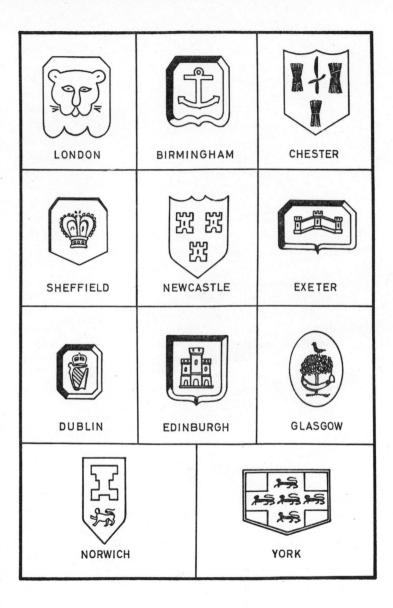

LONDON

BIRMINGHAM

CHESTER

SHEFFIELD

NEWCASTLE

EXETER

DUBLIN

EDINBURGH

GLASGOW

NORWICH

YORK

Silver Plate made in Great Britain and Ireland for a few shillings. (If you are a customer and the jeweller has a kind heart he may even present you with a copy free.) Like a schoolboy's "crib" this will do your translations for you and be invaluable. But—it does not give the maker's names. For this extra information you must consult the indispensable "Jackson".

"Jackson" is an expensive tome. There are not innumerable copies to be had, since it is much sought after, as you can understand. You may have to wait for your copy. In your early days you may not want to incur the expense of buying it. Remember that every first-class dealer has his copy and, free of charge, he will always look up maker's initials for you on request.

In the antique world dealers realise that they exist to help both regular and prospective customers. There is a very fine freemasonry between the antique-dealer and his public. He realises that his customers have to learn from him and he from them. So do not be afraid to ask to look up "Jackson" or for other information you may require.

With this assistance and your little guide you may manage successfully for years with little cost to yourself. The pocket guide will give you the order of reigning sovereigns amongst other information.

Now you are well equipped to start. The number of domestic articles in silver is legion. Suppose you make a humble beginning (as I did) with some small antique silver box, say a vinaigrette or a snuff-box. Choose as good a specimen as you can find. This will give you at least one perfect possession at the outlay of very few pounds indeed. Look at a large number before making a choice. Other points being equal, choose the one you like best and admire most.

Even among Georgian snuff-boxes, fashion prevails. The

oblong flat specimens of a certain size, 3 inches or so, are more esteemed and expensive than smaller, larger or differently shaped kinds. The reason is not far to seek. When I tell you that these particular boxes are known as "cigarette-size" today, the secret is out. They have their modern adaptation for holding cigarettes, either in the pocket or on a table.

When you proffer a cigarette from such a box, if your friend is observant he is pretty sure to exclaim: "What a lovely silver box!"

"Yes," you answer nonchalantly. "Antique, of course. Made by Nathaniel Mills, at Birmingham. In the reign of King George the Third, 1808." Your friend is startled and looks at you with a new respect mingled with suspicion.

"But how can you possibly know all that about it?"

"Simple, my dear fellow," you answer, in the tone of Sherlock Holmes educating his obtuse friend Dr. Watson. "Look at the various hall-marks stamped inside the box. They tell me all that."

Your friend is awed. He realises that you have knowledge and taste which he has not. To your unsophisticated friend you are a connoisseur and an authority. He respects you. This recognition by others of your achievements at an early stage in your career as a collector is not the least of the minor pleasures of collecting.

However, you will not want to remain long at the humble stage of possessing a single object. You may want another vinaigrette or snuff-box, perhaps for yourself or to give away (they make appreciated gifts). Or your wife may be thinking of your hobby in relationship to the home.

A fine pair of Georgian silver candlesticks—George the First, Second, Third or Fourth—looks very well on the dining-table in the evening and on the mantelpiece, sideboard or elsewhere by day. Things of beauty indeed! Bought reasonably today, they are a good investment to-morrow. There is everything to be said in their favour and nothing against them if they are fine, well-marked specimens in good condition.

Or a Georgian silver tea-pot will certainly delight your family and add to the pleasure of five o'clock. If your purse permits, you may desire to have a matching cream-jug, sugar-basin and hot-water-jug and even a silver tea-tray.

Note my word "matching". That is important. It means of the same style and date at least. If by the same maker, all the better. You may not be able to attain your "complete set" at once, either because your purse will not allow or because the dealer from whom you bought in the first instance has not the complete set. This apparent disadvantage often turns out to be the opposite. After a search you may "pick up" in different places at different prices single bargains. Single pieces cost less than the same pieces in a complete set. Besides, when you have completed your set, it may be worth much more, as a set, than you paid for the individual pieces.

Here again is an advantage of being a collector with knowledge and good sense, even with a limited purse. It is the wealthy ignoramus who buys blindly as a shop offers.

A coffee-pot or chocolate-pot, from any time between Queen Anne and Queen Victoria is a lovely—but I must warn you—expensive thing. If you indulge in one you may comfort yourself by reflecting that values in such objects tend to rise with the years, not fall. Fine specimens do not merely keep their value, they have steadily gone up in the past and are doing so in the present. It is difficult to believe that, with more purchasers than ever desiring them, they will decline in value in the future.

Should you find antique coffee-pots and chocolate-pots

beyond your resources, there are less expensive things of antique silver that you may acquire. A pleasant sight in any bedroom is a chamber candlestick made in Georgian or Victorian silver. It can be useful, too. Such a piece is not relatively dear.

Or what is wrong with that delightful article, a silver tankard out of which beer or cider tastes so much better? The Georgian specimens are really beautiful. One for the master of the house, at least, is worth while, and a set would be ideal for guests. Once more, see that the styles, dates and maker coincide.

You may like a Georgian salver for the hall. One could go on specifying desirable silver antiques. There are cups (with covers or not), beakers, flagons, monteiths (or wine-coolers), punch-bowls and ladles, wine cisterns, coolers and toasters, tea-canisters, silver tea-kettles and stands. Also ewers and basins, salt-cellars, sugar-castors, tureens for soup or sauce, dishes, plates and trays, cake-baskets, candelabra, cutlery, inkstands—all fine examples of the silver-smith's art. My list will be more than enough for the amateur to go on with, but it does not pretend to be exhaustive.

Speaking of silversmiths, it is time to say that there are great, and lesser, ones. By common consent, the greatest of all is Paul de Lamerie. A Lamerie piece is for million-aires. Paul Storr, a later worker, is also highly esteemed, but nothing like Lamerie. Then there is a craze for the work by Peter, Hester or Ann Bateman—especially Hester. They are, it seems, specially sought after by American buyers merely it is sometimes said of Hester and Ann, because women silversmiths of old were rare. There are a number of silversmiths whose style is sufficiently indi-vidual even for the amateur to be able to recognise it after seeing a few specimens. A Samuel Pemberton or a Nathaniel

Mills, for example. However, many are indistinguishable, at first glance, even by the elect.

You will progress to a point where you desire to go deeper into the fascinating subject of antique silver. An excellent up-to-date book at a cheap price is *Silver*, by Gerald Taylor. It costs only 5*s*. in the Pelican series. A thoroughly sound treatise on its subject, many beginners may find it rather hard going. I can commend the illustrations, which will teach the beginner the appearance of pieces more quickly and permanently than volumes of description.

One of the things about antique gold and silver is their comparative freedom from fakes. This simplifies the task of the would-be buyer, since he does not have to be so constantly and vigilantly on his guard, as in the case of old china or furniture. There are heavy penalties for counterfeiting assay-marks. The possessor of a forged piece is liable to have his property destroyed. Not that instances of fakes and forgeries in these precious metals are unknown, but in gold they are very rare indeed, and in silver fairly so.

What is generally done to defraud genuine old silver, attested by its hall-marks, is this: The faker acquires a modern reproduction of a fine, large old piece, fakes it a little, and lets into it an old date-letter and hall-marks. In themselves these marks are perfect and genuine, since the forger has cut them out of a genuine little-worth small piece (such as an old spoon). By a skilled worker, this letting-in of an old bit of silver into a modern piece can be done so that the "let-in" is imperceptible to the naked eye.

The next thing is to "let in" the guileless buyer!

So hall-marks and their surround should always be examined with a powerful magnifying-glass. This is calculated to show up even skilful and artistic faking. Another good precaution is to look closely at the workmanship, for the modern work is seldom as good as the ancient. That indeed always should be done. If the marks are not "let in" but simulated by a modern false stamp, the workmanship is the best safeguard.

However, there are far fewer counterfeits in gold and silver at the present day than might be supposed. The danger is not a very important one for the beginner. Small articles (except Apostles' spoons, Carolean sugar-dredgers and so forth, which fetch large sums) were too cheap once for counterfeiting their kind to pay the faker. Small silver articles are, in general, immune from the forger's attentions.

From their precious character, gold and silver articles deserve the greatest care. As everybody knows, silver easily tarnishes, and from time to time must be cleaned. Harsh abrasives used by servants have obliterated valuable marks and in the past reduced the value of many a fine piece. Faint marks indeed are almost always a sign of repeated bad cleanings, which also reduce the weight of the precious metal. Gold of high carat is particularly soft and needs sensible treatment. It may therefore be useful if I give what few households know: the best and safest way of cleaning and preserving gold and silver.

Gold: Wash the article in a weak solution of liquid ammonia or eau de Cologne and water. Polish with a soft cloth. Gold requires the gentlest handling.

Silver Gilt: Never use brushes or patent abrasive cleansers. Paul de Lamerie's words, modernised, are approved by modern opinion: "Clean it with only warm water and soap, using a sponge and then wash with clean water. Dry with a soft linen cloth. Keep it in a dry place, for the damp will spoil it."

Silver: If in continual use and care this should not need

more than very warm soap or detergent and water. Rinse thoroughly and dry with a soft cloth or chamois-leather. If corroded, use the red powder known as "jewellers' rouge". For ornamental parts, use a soft brush with ammonia and chalk.

Remember that salt corrodes silver badly, so give special attention to silver salt-cellars. Sulphur also attacks silver, so you should never use silver spoons with eggs—do so, and you will see why at once. Remember that most tap-water today contains chlorine, which discolours silver, so silver should never be left wet.

If you store your silver, wrap it in acid-free tissue-paper. The traditional way of keeping it in green baize bags is excellent, and it certainly should be protected from the discoloration of damp airs.

*   *   *

In this chapter on antique gold and silver a good deal has been said upon boxes. For box-fanciers (who are numerous and enthusiastic) may be added a word of help to those who cannot afford antique gold or silver, but are fascinated by boxes in general. Antique snuff- and other boxes are to be found in tortoiseshell, boxwood, thuringa wood, sycamore, pewter, horn, papiermâché, porcelain and other materials. Some of these are of little value and may be picked up for two or three shillings, or even less. On the other hand, if you come across a papiermâché box with the name of that master-decorator "Samuel Raven" inscribed under the cover in red script, that is a very valuable article indeed. A porcelain box can also be a thing of great price, as well as exquisite beauty.

While on the subject of boxes, there is one special type of antique silver box that is rather out of fashion and tending to be cheaper than the more usual specimens. It is a box ornamented with Niello work and generally called a niello box. This is silver incised, i.e. cut into ornamental patterns, the lines being filled with a black metallic substance made of mixed silver, copper, lead and sulphur. The black pattern is the point. Often the box is either Russian or French—the Russian generally being less fine than the French box.

Perhaps it is the black appearance which renders this box less popular? I have one that copies a Teniers picture in niello on the outside lid, and a very fine box it is.

4

Old Sheffield Plate

WHAT exactly is Sheffield Plate?

It is a term of art—as it may have been in Birmingham—and is used to denote articles made of copper coated with silver by a special process. That process has now been lost, and electro-plating taken its place. This silver-plated work of Hanoverian days was made from 1760 to about 1836, when the discovery of quicker and cheaper electro-plating killed it commercially. Deservedly upon its very real merits, Old Sheffield Plate has become highly esteemed as a very fashionable subject for collectors.

It began as a cheap substitute for real silver plate. Today, after a period of disfavour, it has once more become what it was intended to be by its craftsmen: a worthy rival to hand-wrought silver. Quite as much time, labour and skill were expended upon it as upon silver manufacture. As might be expected, genuine pieces of "Old Sheffield" in good condition have beauty and distinction enough to keep them appreciating in value. In price, fine specimens often exceed their counterparts in modern silver, and rightly so.

In appearance, Old Sheffield Plate equals solid silver. Yet it does not look exactly the same to the educated eye. Old Sheffield has a special soft sheen, a peculiar lustre subtly different from the brilliance of solid silver. The distinction is not easy to explain in words, but it is quite discernible to the eye of the careful observer. You do not need to put Sheffield side by side with silver to detect it.

Personally I would say that the satiny sheen of Sheffield is somewhat gentler, quieter, the veriest trifle less dazzling, than the harder brightness of silver. Enthusiastic Sheffield Plate collectors declare their preference for this muted brilliance or special lustre. Careless observers may not even notice it and often proclaim a piece of Sheffield to be silver, until informed otherwise. However, the difference in appearance though slight is real enough, and ordinary people quickly educate their eyes to see it.

If the article happens to be much worn, damaged or badly silvered at its making, the underlying copper may show through in places. This is very much to the disparagement and devaluation of the article. Therefore, always examine a piece of Sheffield Plate for any trace of copper showing through, on a worn place.

While it is true that Sheffield Plate is essentially silver fused over copper, if you see any piece in a dealer's shop-window marked "Silver plated on copper" (as you often do), this means that the article is not Old Sheffield Plate but merely electro-plate of a later date. This legend, like the legend "Solid Gold" of English jewellers' shops, often misleads the unwary. Dealers generally know the importance and value of Sheffield Plate, and usually take care to mark it as such.

The discovery that silver and copper could be united by fusion was first made in 1743 by Thomas Bolsover, a Sheffield cutler. The resulting Sheffield Plate is entirely English in origin. As I have shown, it preceded electro-plate, which was much cheaper to manufacture and which killed the making of Sheffield Plate. Bolsover promptly made buttons, small circular and oval boxes with push-off lids, hand embossed. His apprentice Hancock took the manufacture a stage further in competing with his master. He made a wide range of domestic ware including candlesticks,

47

tea-pots, coffee-pots, hot-water jugs, saucepans and similar articles.

The great name in Sheffield Plate, however, is that of Matthew Boulton, who came into the business at Birmingham in 1760. To Sheffield Plate he is what Paul de Lamerie is to silver. In five years he had formed the Matthew Boulton Plate Company—that name and its founders, as well as Boulton and Watt, are to be eagerly looked for by collectors on many articles. From his factory he issued an ever-growing list of manufactures in Sheffield Plate.

Catalogues of Sheffield Plate makers are to be found in the Victoria and Albert Museum and are worthy of attention. The earliest, dating from about 1790, is that of John Green of Sheffield, another of 1797 by John Cadman, also of Sheffield, is to be seen there. These catalogues are useful, showing the amateur the range of articles he may expect to find made in Sheffield Plate.

There is a great range of Sheffield Plate. With no attempt to be entirely comprehensive, the following list shows what may be found by collectors in this medium:

Tea-urns, tea and coffee sets or single pieces, cake-baskets, hot-water jugs, tea-caddies, tankards, beakers, bottle-labels, waiters and trays, cruet-stands, toasters, breakfast dishes and covers, soup tureens, chamber candlesticks and other candlesticks, candelabra, wax-taper holders, snuffers and trays, toast racks, standishes, epergnes, wine funnels, salt cellars, spoons and forks, fish-servers, sauce-boats, sauce-tureens, tumbler-stands, entrée-dishes, egg-cups, mustards, sugar-basins, table-heaters and stands, ladles, caddy-spoons, oil-bottle-stands, muffiners, bells, wine-coolers, saucepans, cream-jugs, argyles, strainers and plate-covers.

From this list there can be selected articles to suit every purpose and purse.

A table by Chippendale. Note the ball-and-claw legs

A room of Hepplewhite furniture

Helmet rosewater ewer, made in 1721

Worcester china tea set

Some Sheffield Plate is marked; some unmarked. The unmarked may include many most magnificent specimens. These speak for themselves and need no marks to proclaim their authenticity. Their beauty and extraordinary workmanship tell everything essential at first glance. In such pieces the absence of marking does not matter. Many of the lesser pieces do not speak for themselves, and if unmarked, it is necessary for the collector, early in his career, to know the tests for Sheffield Plate.

The first test involves using a good magnifying-glass. Look closely with it for seams or joins, perhaps invisible to the naked or spectacled eye. The reason is this: period pieces plated on copper were made from separate units. So if no seams or joins can be detected by close examination with the glass, it may safely be assumed that it is not Old Sheffield Plate. It is pretty certain to be a piece of electro-plate, the joints being concealed beneath the film of electrically deposited silver.

Texture and colour of metal are the next important points. The surface-texture and colour are very different in Sheffield Plate and the later electro-plated article. In the latter, minute particles of silver are deposited on the copper, producing a crystalline coating. Close inspection will show that the silver has undergone transmutation, making both colour and texture different from Sheffield plating.

Tests are unnecessary where the Sheffield Plate has its identifying marks. Up to 1784 it was illegal to put any name or mark upon Sheffield Plate. Consequently the earliest pieces are unmarked. In 1784 platers "within 100 miles of Sheffield" were allowed to put their name, number or emblem on each piece. These marks were registered at the Sheffield Assay Office. This continued until 1836. Sheffield registered 55 marks and Birmingham 77.

In spite of this concession of free advertisement a number

of platers and plating-firms continued to turn out their pieces unmarked. Yet strange to say, some of the unmarked ware was better than the marked; and some of the unmarked was indeed first-rate both in design and in quality of workmanship. Perhaps this is partly accounted for by the fact that the Birmingham men hated to register in Sheffield and protested against it for forty years.

After 1820 a crown—the distinctive mark for the town of Sheffield—also could be put on Sheffield Plate. This was to protect the English platers from imported imitations from the Continent. Some platers also began to put on a stamp, indicating the proportion of silver used as against copper.

After 1836, the beginning of Victoria's reign, the Sheffield platers were no longer required to register, but some platers went on striking marks and some naughty men began to strike their plate with marks so closely resembling silver marks as to be calculated to deceive. Even now such pieces, with their imitation of the "lion passant", might take in the careless and unwary. Not, however, the careful observer, warned to use his magnifying-glass.

Should you forget to carry your magnifying-glass and be looking at the mark on Sheffield Plate (or silver or gold for that matter), breathe on the metal immediately before examining it. Blurred by the moisture of your breath, the mark will show up much more clearly. *Crede experto:* trust one who has tried. Professionals and the knowledgeable always do this. Also, while noting marks, fix your main attention on intrinsic merit.

In collecting Sheffield Plate, be on your guard against articles described not as "Sheffield Plate" but as "Sheffield Plated". Only a little "d", but what a difference it makes! Without the "d" it is genuine Sheffield Plate and antique; with the "d" it is likely to be more or less modern electroplate possibly made in Sheffield. This is a trick to overcome the law which makes it an offence to describe any ware as Sheffield Plate which is not the genuine article.

If you want to see some really fine articles in Sheffield Plate—and you most certainly should not miss looking at some—choose any of Matthew Boulton's work; tea-urns bearing the mark of Roberts, Cadman & Company; or one of the same company's elaborately chased trays. Cake-baskets, especially some of the most costly, can be truly described as magnificent of their kind; so can many wine-coolers and entrée-dishes. A three-piece Regency tea-set in Sheffield Plate often leaves nothing to be desired in beauty of design and ornament.

Smaller pieces of their kind also are excellent. Candle-sticks give enormous choice to the collector. It is said that the number of designs is beyond computation, even though definite trends of fashion are followed. A single Sheffield firm in its 28 years is reputed to have issued no fewer than 1,190 distinct patterns of candlestick. It sounds incredible, but illustrates the extraordinary range of choice before the collector. There is also a great diversity of tea-pots in Sheffield Plate.

A word should be said upon gilding. The outside of Sheffield Plate was rarely, if ever, gilded, but certain articles were regularly gilded *inside* as a protection against the chemical action of the contents. Such articles as salt-cellars, mustard-pots, sugar-basins, cream-jugs and so forth were likely to corrode, producing black spots, hard to eliminate. In tea-services the tea-pot might be gilded to match. Gild-ing therefore is not (as is sometimes thought) a mark of not very genuine Sheffield Plate.

There are two disadvantages to Sheffield Plate. Like silver, it requires constantly cleaning, and that means wear. Unlike silver, in course of time, hard wear or too much acid-cleaning, the base metal shows through. Replating may have been done when that has happened. How is the amateur to detect Sheffield Plate which has been replated during (say) Victorian or—still worse—later times?

That problem often arises, and requires solution.

Victorian replating may have toned down with many years' wear and cleaning until it resembles the original. Now fused Sheffield is much harder than electro-plate, and the tinge helps. Sheffield has a faintly bluish tinge, the electro-plated is always whitish. There is a regular trade, and has been since 1849, in "doctoring up" old worn Sheffield Plate by replating over a copper-showing.

Wire-work in Sheffield Plate is known. Amongst the rarest examples are pieces, often basket-style, made from plated wires dating chiefly from 1785 to 1815. These wire-work pieces, like other pierced work of Sheffield Plate, are exceedingly skilful and well contrived. Both for this reason and their rarity, they enjoy special favour.

Sheffield Plate is an extraordinarily good subject for the amateur and the beginner to learn. Confined as it is to one short period, the subject is not complicated. Real "Sheffield" is not difficult to identify and one soon learns to detect replating or restoration. Then the purchase cost is not prohibitive. The lesser articles are cheap enough. Though the early pieces fetch very good prices, these are far below their counterparts in silver of the same period. The period was one of good taste and the Sheffield platers deliberately followed the designs of the best goldsmiths and silversmiths. The result is seen in the fact that it is almost impossible to overpraise the beauty and elegance of some of the fine pieces of Sheffield Plate available to the private collector today.

A special question beginners ask about "Old Sheffield" is this: "If I find a fine piece at a reasonable or low price, should I abstain from buying it because at one point or perhaps two the copper is showing through?" For my own part I would say that there is so much to be had in fine condition that I personally would not touch the imperfect. Still, this is not every collector's view so far as Sheffield Plate is concerned if the blemish is trifling. Perhaps collectors less stringent and difficult than myself may prefer to be guided by their own notion of whether they are likely to come across a similar but perfect piece, next month or next year.

Just as Sheffield Plate was sometimes made at Birmingham so, for a time, some of it was made in France, Holland and Russia, which countries took the cue from England. In general, this foreign Sheffield Plate is of inferior quality to the English and may be ignored by the amateur.

Collectors of Sheffield Plate find their hobby fascinating. As the field is a severely limited one, they are apt to wish to know all about it. There are not many books devoted solely to the subject, but the classic is *Sheffield Plate*, by Henry Newton Veitch (1908). Apart from its authoritative character, it has abundant illustrations and contains a list of makers' names and their marks. Though written more than half a century ago, the book remains a "must" for every collector determined to be an expert upon its subject.

5

Pewter, Pinchbeck—and Baxters

FROM gold, silver and Sheffield Plate, to come to what are commonly called "base metals" seems something of an anticlimax. But from an aesthetic point of view, the gleam of copper vessels in a kitchen, or a brass warming-pan against oak panelling in the right sort of hall, can be delightful. Even dull lead in the shape of a carved and dated cistern in the garden looks well indeed.

Pewter—most satiny-grey amalgam of metals—is not to everybody's liking. Devotees of silver and "Old Sheffield" are often impervious to its charm, yet it has its enthusiasts. In a suitable setting, alongside old oak in a cottage or tavern, it can be highly attractive. Collectors of English, Scottish, French, German, Flemish or American pewter are numerous: indeed, the cult is world-wide. That most celebrated of all pewterers, François Briot, is as famous as any other artist in metals.

Pewter-collecting is no declining hobby, and can be instructive as well as valuable and interesting. As in other lines, fine, graceful and rare pieces exist. In England the records of the Worshipful Company of Pewterers go back to 1348, the time of Edward the Third, so that there is plenty of scope for research.

Of course, pewter is much older than Plantagenet times. In Britain it was used in Roman days: long before ancient Rome, China and Japan knew it. In Britain it succeeded leather and horn—both obtained from animals—and at first pewter was possessed only by great nobles and ecclesiastics. In the seventeenth century there was hardly a vessel or utensil of any description in tavern, church or house that was not made in the metal.

If you mean to collect a quantity of old English pewter, selection is very necessary. You can choose "sad ware"; the pewterers' name for plates, dishes and chargers. Or you might choose "hollow ware"; such as flagons, tankards, beakers and such pieces. On the other hand you may confine yourself to one article, such as spoons. Or, alternatively, collect a diversity of pieces like candlesticks, inkstands, saltcellars and so forth. Or even specialise in tavern, household or ecclesiastical pieces.

Pewter consists of tin mixed with an alloy of other metal, generally lead. Antique pewter varies a good deal in its composition, and may have copper or lead as its alloy. To test the quality of your pewter, rub it with a clean piece of white paper:

No mark: Means a proportion of 90 parts of tin to 10 of lead.
Faint marks: Means 75 parts of tin to 25 of lead.

Of course, the heavier the mark on rubbing, the greater the proportion of lead in the pewter. The greater the quantity of tin, the better the pewter. This table is only an approximation for purchasers to test the quality of their pewter. Between the two criteria given above, in the nature of things, the test can be no more accurate than fair guesswork.

The chief charm of old pewter lies in its soft grey colour, which attracts a *patina* that time alone gives. Another attraction lies in its proportions and functional fitness. These four things: colour, form, alloy-quality tested as by the method of the above paragraph, and fitness for its purpose are what the collector should consider in making a purchase.

In olden times in England and in Scotland, each pewterer of any standing in his craft had his "touch", or private mark, which was registered. It might consist of his name and a rose, a figure, or an animal or other device. Guilds of pewterers in their day strictly regulated the craft, as the Board of Trade, for weights and measures purposes, still does to a lesser extent.

Consequently collectors of the antique can find the approximate date of many pieces by making themselves familiar with the marks. Antique pewter calls for nearly as much detailed knowledge as gold or silver. Therefore the beginner should not rush to buy before studying the subject. This is best done by first getting Mr. A. V. Sutherland-Graeme's little handbook on the subject, *Old British Pewter* (*1500 to 1800*), published by *The Connoisseur* (1951). Then chat with knowledgeable dealers (though it must be admitted that few have very specialised knowledge), visit museums and the rare pewter-specialists such as those two famous shops in the Brompton Road.

Compared with other antiques, pewter prices are low and many attractive pieces are picked up for a pound or less in out-of-the-way shops. Yet pewter-prices can reach three figures for a single article, though the market for them is obviously a limited one.

A word must be said about what I call bastard-pewter, known as "Britannia metal". Both in composition and appearance it is, indeed, a kind of debased pewter. Hard and cold looking, a dead dull colourless metal, any article made of it has nothing of the *patina*, the sheen and gleam, of genuine old pewter or the high artificial polish of modern pewter.

You have only to place two objects side by side, one

made of Britannia metal and the other of genuine good-class pewter—i.e. pewter with a high proportion of tin in it—to see, learn and know the difference for ever. My advice? Regard it as inferior in every way, of little value, but sometimes over-priced in the shops.

*　　　*　　　*

In common talk, pinchbeck is a word of reproach indicating a mean, low imitation of the real thing. But in the world of antiques, pinchbeck is not always to be despised. It has its place and its enthusiastic fanciers.

What exactly is pinchbeck? Between the years 1670 and 1766 two brothers, Christopher and Edward Pinchbeck, were making what they called "toys" for grown-ups. These comprised widely differing objects: sword-belts, hangers, whip-handles, cane-heads, watch-chains, coat-buttons, salvers, snuff-boxes, patch-boxes, shoe-buckles, necklaces, clasps, all sorts of buckles, watch-cases, etuis (small cases generally containing implements), chatelaines (for suspending clusters of useful things from the girdle or belt), miniature frames, rings, bracelets, jewellery set with the cheaper gems, and dozens of others too numerous to mention.

All this was done for those who could not afford "the real thing". Both male and female servants wanted to be like their finely adorned masters and mistresses; the trading classes wanted to vie in appearance with their "betters", the professionals and the aristocracy. So the Pinchbeck brothers imitated very closely and skilfully the real thing: chiefly gold, and did it very well indeed. Their old pinchbeck was so carefully and knowledgeably made and worked upon as to be elaborately artistic. Christopher, in fact, also had made a new and original discovery: how to make an alloy with cheap copper and zinc that closely counterfeited gold. It could be embossed, chased and stamped to look very pretty and at a glance, mistaken for real gold. The Pinchbeck brothers had some secret that has been lost— no one, by mixing copper and zinc, can make pinchbeck of their quality today.

Old pinchbeck has something of quality the latter lacks. That is the secret of its fascination for modern collectors of antiques.

If you cannot afford to pay between twenty and fifty pounds for a fine Georgian silver snuff-box—or less for a patch-box, bon-bon box or a vinaigrette—that is no reason why similar non-precious antique boxes should not adorn a table or cabinet in your home. You can have them in pinchbeck. As decorative objects, these are by no means despicable. Often these pieces are very nice indeed. Square, oblong or oval slips of onyx or agate or moss-agate or cairngorm often form the tops or the bottoms of these boxes. The settings of the stones and the sides of the box are of metal that looks like dull, or "matt", gold and often this metal is finely chased and decorated. Of course, the metal is not even gold-plated. It is pinchbeck.

Such pieces can often be picked up for a very few shillings. Take care they are *old* pinchbeck, for strange to say imitation has been achieved—especially by the Swiss, who admired it enough for that. This modern "pinchbeck" is not so good as the old as you will soon come to realise.

The Pinchbeck brothers claimed for their wares that they were untarnishable—a high claim indeed. It is only fair to add that much old pinchbeck has remained untarnished to this very day. A great deal, however, has dulled and darkened under the chemical influences of the polluted atmospheres over a century or so.

You will understand from all this why pinchbeck is collected and not looked down upon. Certain articles are particularly attractive: the ring and jewel caskets. These may be found in red agate, white agate, moss-agate, lapis-lazuli and onyx; sometimes they are in a mosaic of such stones. They are dainty articles on which skill and care was lavished and well deserve preservation. So the ordinary meaning of the word "pinchbeck"—a pretence and a sham—does not really apply to old pinchbeck, which is a lost art. You might do worse than to collect a few fine specimens of pinchbeck.

I cannot promise you that it is a money-maker. It could even be a money-loser, for it is the sort of thing that might easily go entirely out of fashion. As against that, you may safely reflect that any loss will be small—as will any profit. Of course, if pinchbeck suddenly became fashionable . . . as unlikely things *have* happened! Look at glass paper-weights. Once they were broken up, thrown away or handed to children to play with. Now there is a world-wide cult of them, with correspondingly high prices.

For my part I have only one piece of pinchbeck—but what a beauty! As a collector of fine gold and silver I smiled at pinchbeck for a long time, but when I saw this box, I fell for it. Its top, bottom and side-panels are an exquisite mosaic and its supporting pieces of pinchbeck look like fine gold, superbly chased. In a cabinet, or even in the hand, this cigarette-sized deep box is a ravishing sight. In appearance it equals, nay even excels, many a gold and enamel box. For this treasure (which I could not resist) I paid £5 in days when that was considered a substantial sum of money. I thought that irresistible box dear at the time I bought it—but have never thought so since. It has given me years of pleasure, and now I see the prospect of a profit, if I wanted one. So genuine old pinchbeck is worth considering from the aesthetic point of view, even if no immediate fortune lies in it.

There is a general moral in all this applicable to antique-collecting in general. In following the broad highways do not despise the by-ways, bridle-paths and footpaths of collecting. What you have learned about pinchbeck, after gold and silver, also applies to other subjects, such as Baxter oil-colour prints, after Old and Modern Masters. To a great collector of fine oil-paintings and water-colours, a Baxter print may seem uninteresting and below his lordly regard. Yet such prints are esteemed, attract goodish prices and are worthy of close attention. Unfortunately, just as the secret of the Pinchbecks died with them, so did Baxter's die with him.

It is indeed fortunate that we do not all want or need to collect the same things. A metal such as pinchbeck may seem a world away from a Baxter oil-print, but from the collecting point of view, different though they appear, they follow a similar pattern.

George Baxter was a remarkable man who died in 1867. His oil-colour prints are avidly sought today and have been for many years now. On their merits they well deserve to be. Baxter prints were the frontispieces and vignettes of many books in the 1840's and '50's. One of the earliest—possibly the very earliest—illustrated *The Feathered Tribes* in 1834. In addition Baxter issued numerous portraits of celebrities and others about $4\frac{1}{2}$ inches long by 3 inches wide. Some of these rank amongst his best work. The popularity of his prints created another demand: for pictures pure and simple by him. He fulfilled that demand.

The fact that oil-colour prints like Baxter's now cannot be produced—his secret having died with him—adds both to their rarity and value. Again, his illustrations were liked so much by children and others that they were often torn out of old, unwanted volumes, pasted into scrapbooks and later destroyed. Fortunately for our generation, Baxter had a voluminous output.

How can you recognise a Baxter and tell whether it is worth acquiring?

You should note the following points. (1) It should be clean and unfaded. (2) Show good margins or mounts. (3) The imprint of the name and address of Baxter should be at a bottom corner of the picture, embossed in white, or stamped in red on the margin or mount. The legend was usually: "Printed in Oil Colours by Geo. (or G) Baxter", "Patentee", followed by one of his business addresses. There were four: First 29 King Square, next 3 Charterhouse Square, then 11 Northampton Square, and finally 11 & 12 Northampton Square. Baxter had licensees, the chief being (1) Le Blond, (2) Kronheim, (3) Bradshaw & Blacklock. Licensees' work may have their names printed, but their work is always inferior to a real "Baxter" in colour, finish and tone. Sometimes in early days Le Blond used Baxter's name. Later he used his own and Le Blond prints, though of less esteem, are often collected.

Baxter's work methods have been freely written about, and enthusiasts delight in studying them. In the full sense of the word Baxter was a very great artist. His work is unique and likely to remain so—hence its reputation. It is not my purpose to relate his highly technical methods here, even if they are fully and accurately known (which I gravely doubt), yet they are often described.

What was this secret of his that eludes discovery? It has been suggested that it was the composition of his colours. Again, it is said to lie in extreme conscientiousness and attention to minute detail in engraving. Certainly he used the very best colours and paper. Le Blond uses smooth thin paper, but Baxter's is very different. Still, one doubts if these materials could account for all that difference. Perhaps much of his excellence came from his ability: his great love of taking pains, and the fact that he never delegated his work, from its first to its last stage. Anyhow, no contemporary or subsequent process of colour-printing attained his standard.

Locate a *Baxter Book Catalogue*, then search for one or two of the hundred odd works that he illustrated. (There is a complete list in Courtney Lewis's book entitled *George Baxter*.) Do not succumb to the temptation to tear out the picture and frame it merely because the letterpress itself is rubbishy stuff (as it may be). The books are to be treasured intact, not for their literary merits but for the Baxter illustration. Indeed, "Baxter" books in themselves make a special "line" for collecting. Believe it or not, there was a time when Baxter oil-prints could be picked up for about eighteen-pence. Today you will generally have to pay a few pounds.

Naturally forgeries and fakes abound. Baxter's greatest masterpiece, "The Descent from the Cross", is a favourite victim. Again, the prints of Baxter's licensees often deceive. It is fair to say that much of the work of Le Blond, Kronheim and others has personal merit. Not that the result is a true Baxter. Le Blond probably approached him more closely than any other man, but place a Le Blond and a Baxter side by side and usually you can see at a glance that the former is defective in brilliancy of colour. Neither does it compare in beauty with the work of the Master. "Baxters" are no longer in their heyday for high prices, but will come back, for their intrinsic excellence is beyond dispute.

6

Tea, Coffee and Chocolate Sets

IN dealing with the general subject of silver, brief reference
has been made to the collection of tea- or coffee-sets. So
popular and rewarding is this kind of useful collecting that
it needs to be dealt with in more detail. Home-lovers of
both sexes take a special pride and pleasure in it.

Besides, antiques connected with tea, coffee or chocolate
drinking have always offered a large, varied and most interesting field to the collector. They have the advantage of
being practical and of everyday use. At a moderate ex-
penditure and by taking a little time and trouble, the
ordinary beginner can acquire a fine collection of table
appointments.

If expense is of no matter, you will express your taste in
silver. An antique silver tea-tray of the Georgian period is
a lovely thing indeed, especially when accompanied by a
silver tea-pot and stand, a silver cream-ewer, hot-water jug,
sugar-basin, cake-basket, tea-caddy (or better still a set of
them) with a silver caddy-spoon—and even a silver tea-
kettle and spirit stand. If they are all by the same maker
and from the same year, you have a complete and rare
treasure. Of its kind, this is perfection, but almost unat-
tainable, except at considerable expense after a long period
of years of collecting. You may lessen the expense by sub-
stituting a salver or waiter for the tray and cutting out
such an extra as the tea-kettle. Without seeking that all-
silver perfection (no gold service of that character is known)

you can put together a very satisfying, useful set of antiques for the tea-table. Let us see what can be done.

Tea-pots can be had not only in antique silver but in Sheffield Plate, porcelain and pottery. Tea-caddies are obtainable in many metals and woods of varying degrees of craftsmanship, also in tortoiseshell and papiermâché. Caddy spoons can be bought in innumerable shapes and sizes. I do not recommend them of base metal, while silver ones are so reasonable in price, besides, the china ones are often preferred. Cream-jugs, sugar-bowls, sweetmeat-dishes are to be had in china as well as silver. Complete tea-services of the most decorative character from the old factories of Bow, Derby, Chelsea, Bristol, Worcester or Liverpool, Caughley, New Hall, Rockingham and Davenport are to be picked up, piecemeal, at reasonable figures. Complete sets are far from cheap. It is not really difficult to assemble, bit by bit, over a reasonable period of time, such a tea-table as will be a source of pride to the household and delight to visitors.

As an alternative, you might collect a satisfying, elegant coffee-set. Start with a Georgian silver salver or tray. Add a Georgian or Queen Anne coffee-pot (value, three figures) with its twin ewer and twin sugar-basin for the filling of fine porcelain coffee-cups and saucers. The whole will look very impressive.

If you decide to do this—to attain what I may call the antique tea- or coffee-table complete—let me interpolate one or two warnings.

First of all, do not aim at a heterogeneous collection. Secondly, do not buy imperfect pieces, however tempting their cheapness. A cracked and mended piece of china is not for the serious collector. The chipped, damaged or imperfect china, the bent or battered silver, become an eyesore with further acquaintance. Do not be tempted. There is neither intrinsic nor decorative value and the imperfect is nowhere so out of place as upon a tea-table.

However, such a complete set, still usable, may not appeal to you. You might prefer to make a collection of one subject when your first step is to choose your article. There are objects which are unsuitable for collecting. It is safe to say that no one has ever made a collection of scullery-sinks or kitchen-fenders, except by way of trade. While it is very nice to possess a tea-kettle—in particular I would say a Queen Anne tea-kettle complete with lamp and stand which would be cheap at £500—a museum is the right place for a vast collection of tea-kettles. Certain smaller objects make a satisfying collection. I would instance tea-caddy spoons. They delight many collectors.

Dated from about the year 1780, you can pick them up in fine condition and all shapes and sizes. You can easily acquire a hundred or so, all different—in the Victoria and Albert Museum they have over 200. This exceptional collection is well worth looking at. Often you can trace the year by the stamped date-letter; sometimes even the maker and the town of manufacture. These attractive little silver trifles are found in all sorts of forms, from vine-leaves to jockey caps, and they are generally most beautifully made.

The tea-caddy itself fascinates many people. Fine specimens are eagerly snapped up, while broken-down and "restored" specimens are common, which shows the popularity of the boxes. You find them in single or multiple sets—the multiples consisting at most of two or three. They may be made of silver, ivory, Sheffield Plate, straw-work, mahogany plain or inlaid, walnut, ebony or maple, as well as in pottery or porcelain.

Single or multiple, the tea-caddy in fine condition can be a most useful, and incidentally lovely, piece of household equipment. Of the wooden ones walnut caddies are perhaps the rarest, but the finest and earliest mahogany ones are by no means common. The greatest cabinet-makers did not disdain the tea-caddy. Sheraton designed very lovely painted and inlaid boxes. The last quarter of the eighteenth century was the time for the finest tea-caddies.

In a way the caddy itself is more of a challenge to the collector than the silver caddy-spoon. While the silver spoon has its marks, the caddy has nothing but its intrinsic excellence to speak for it. It shows its owner's taste and judgment, and its beauty the reason it has been favoured. Even if the wise collector fancies a tea-caddy he will not purchase it, however reasonable the price, unless he is able to say with confidence: "I have seen many caddies and this is definitely one of the finest I have seen. Moreover, it is in perfect condition. Having examined it under a magnifying-glass I am satisfied it has not been 'restored' in any way, but is its original self."

Incidentally, if he is prudent he will not say this aloud! He will invite the dealer's opinion—and his guarantee—and remark that if the price is reasonable, he has a mind to buy it. He will have educated himself upon the current prices of tea-caddies of the kind in which he is interested.

Passing now to the antique chocolate-pot, this very much resembles the coffee-pot. It may surprise you to hear that although chocolate drinking in England is much less popular than tea or coffee drinking, the chocolate-pot commands as high a price as the antique coffee-pot. It must be confessed that antique silver specimens of either are highly expensive. Few of us can afford these luxuries.

7

Millefiore: or Glass Paperweights

OF recent years a considerable craze has developed for collecting millefiore or glass paperweights. The vogue is perhaps rather less today than when ex-King Farouk of Egypt would spend over £1,000 upon a single specimen to add to what was said to be the finest collection in the world. In those days too, Colette, the inimitable French novelist, was more than once photographed with her collection. Collecting these attractive little pieces is still fashionable. While prices can run into three figures for a rare single piece, one may pick up one or two cheaply.

Called millefiore (or thousand flowers) by the Venetians who originated, or rather resurrected them in the eighteenth century, they are said to be a lost art of the ancient Romans. A glass-maker of Murano, who rediscovered them, deserves gratitude, but his very name is forgotten.

What exactly are they? They are shining balls of glass crystal, usually rather larger than an orange or a tennis ball, in which is embedded (a usual example) cunningly devised beds of gaily-coloured flowers. Instead of flowers there may be a snake, a salamander, or a brilliant-hued butterfly, hovering life-sized over a single flower or nosegay. Some millefiores contain portraits.

These objects are most attractive and were a feature of the Great Exhibition of 1851. For a long time after that they fell into neglect and could be acquired for next to nothing. Many fine specimens were given to children as playthings and became broken in the process. However, at last people began to realise their beauty, and the fact that they were genuine masterpieces, most skilfully designed and wrought. Of course they have no long ancestry, being productions of the nineteenth century.

Millefiore reached their acme of perfection in the work of three French factories: St. Louis, Baccarat and Clichy. Signed specimens are so rare as to be almost unknown. These three factories had many copyists and imitators. For that matter, glass paperweights of a cheap imitative sort are plentiful enough. The would-be collector very quickly trains himself to distinguish between the genuine and the spurious. The latter are often so poor and crude, both in colouring and workmanship, that a single glance may suffice to tell. Those who have once looked attentively at a few fine specimens of the real thing will readily reject the copy.

In collecting any form of antique it is always advisable to familiarise one's eye and hand with the actual genuine pieces by looking and touching them. With French glass paperweights this is more than ever necessary. Illustrations, photographic or line-drawings, may be valuable in other cases, but here give an insufficient idea—in some cases—of what the paperweight looks like. The tiny details and faint touches cannot be clearly shown in illustration. These are what speak so eloquently to the observer, who naturally needs to concern himself with these "points". Again, verbal description helps less than usual, for each paperweight may differ subtly from its fellows and have a personal touch of its own.

Like Sheffield Plate, glass paperweights were made during a strictly limited period—always an advantage to a collector—since that means that the knowledge he has to acquire is easily managed. Few subjects are as limited. The best period is indeed short, namely from 1845 to 1849.

Some collectors add a late period, going up to 1875. While we do not know the names of the French craftsmen in this connection, we do know the English name of the famous Ashley Pellatt. Luckily the dates are often clearly marked on the individual piece. The numerals of these dates are coloured in red, blue and green within white cones set in a line. Sometimes you may find a "B" set between the "8" and the "9". These dates are never centralised in genuine specimens. If a date is centralised, the piece should be regarded with suspicion as a fake.

Pieces from the "Clichy" factory are not dated. All Clichy types—and every variety was made there—are marked with a "C". Clichy paperweights have noticeably vivid colours. Sometimes a rose is prominent in the pattern.

St. Louis pieces carry dates from 1845 to 1849 inclusive. This factory was the first to use dates. Its pieces may have S.L. for mark or a reversed S. Often there is a swirl with a point of coloured cones radiating spirally from the top.

Baccarat pieces are found dated from 1846 to 1849. When present, the signature is the initial "B".

Sometimes glass paperweights are known as "French glass paperweights", but the adjective of nationality is a trifle misleading. One English maker—a notable exception —ranks in collecting circles with the French. That is the aforementioned Ashley Pellatt, the great English craftsman whose work is highly distinctive and much prized. It consists of a plaque made of unglazed white china modelled in relief and embedded in the glass receptacle. This results in the plaque showing as a sulphide of bright silver colour.

The advantage of collecting an article in such limited production as glass paperweights has been stressed. These fascinating objects also have another advantage from a modern point of view—they do not take up much space, even when collected in quantity, and are easily portable. They require virtually no cleaning or any other attention, and they can easily be displayed. Nor are they unduly susceptible to damage. All these points are important in modern days when most people live in flats or small houses. Apart from space-restrictions, they must clean their possessions themselves owing to the lack of servants.

If it is not desired to form a really comprehensive collection, the admirer of these objects may still be well advised to pick up one or two good specimens. Their brightness and vivid colouring enable them to form a welcome ornament in almost any room in the house. On a mantelpiece, table, shelf, writing-desk or a window-sill—virtually anywhere you care to put one of them—they add brightness to the vicinity.

Perhaps a word of explanation should be added regarding an often rough, unfinished spot at the base of a glass paperweight which makes the uninitiated in their early collecting career think that this shows bad finish. No collector of old wine-glasses will fall into a similar mistake. He will be familiar with this "pontil-mark" (as it is called) upon cherished old drinking-glasses. The pontil is an iron rod, used by glass-workers, to which the molten glass vessel sticks in the making of the article. When the article is finished, the glass is broken off the rod. The article retains the mark of this breaking off—which is known as the pontil-mark. Rather it is a sign of a piece being genuine than the reverse.

So widespread has become the desire to have one paperweight or more that nowadays you will find these objects in almost every antique-shop in the country. Unfortunately the great majority are modern imitations of no particular merit. We may stress again—for the beginner's peace of mind—that these imitations are unlikely to deceive anyone who takes the trouble to give a few hours to the study of the genuine antique.

There are still enough of the real period pieces about to make a search for them worth while. The old proverb, "Every day is fishing day but not every day is catching day", is to the point here. When a fine product of St. Louis, Baccarat, Clichy or of Ashley Pellatt is found at anything like a reasonable price, it should be eagerly snapped up.

American-market fancy-prices should never be paid, for there is always a risk that over-rated fashionable things may fall out of fashion. In March 1961 a New York dealer paid at Sotheby's in London £700 for a Clichy pink glass paperweight containing a rose in a blue-and-white basket. At the same sale Baccarat prices ran from £130 upwards. At this rate four figures soon may be seen again.

It is equally possible there may be a move in a downward direction, if, on the deaths of their holders, some large collections are suddenly flung on to the market. It should always be borne in mind that there is no intrinsic value in these articles. The price is thoroughly artificial when reaching such heights as those quoted above for what were once the toys of Victorian children in the nursery. On the other hand, the fashion now seems to be well established, especially in the U.S.A., where a learned bulletin on the subject is circulated regularly to paperweight enthusiasts.

The serious collector intending to make a real study of this line will like to know of two sound books: *Paperweight and Other Curiosities*, by E. M. Elville (London, 1954), and *French Crystal Paperweights*, by R. Imbert and Y. Amic (Paris, 1948).

8

Pottery and Earthenware

AT some time everybody has seen a Toby jug. Many humble families proudly cherish a single specimen—"my old Toby jug what Grandfer had", as our Poet Laureate, Dr. John Masefield, expresses it. Real and imitation Tobies exist in large numbers. To the attractiveness of the real the large quantity of imitations is due. Some of the imitations are frank copies, and do not pretend to be anything else. Many others are fakes and forgeries intended to deceive the antique collector, some being skilfully and cunningly executed. It behoves the beginner therefore to be on his guard. The risk of a bad purchase is great.

The original Toby jug is traditionally supposed to be a pot-portrait of:

> *Old Toby Philpot, as thirsty a soul*
> *As e'er drank a bottle or trundled a bowl.*

Learned men say it is a development from the stone-ware wine-flask of a bearded man of the sixteenth and seventeenth centuries called a "Bellarmine", after Cardinal Bellarmine. To judge by Toby's costume, the jug came in during the early eighteenth century, and this accords with what is known. The typical "Toby" shows a short, fat, old fellow with an ale-jug on his knee. Usually he wears a tricorne (a three-cornered hat), but there are a number of varieties.

"The Old English Gentleman" has a refined face, though

he also has his jug and glass. "The Sailor" sits on a chest marked "dollars"; "The Postboy" astride a barrel; "The Hearty Good Fellow" has his Bible at the base of the jug; "The Watchman" holds a lantern; "The Squire" has a three-cornered chair; "The German" a big pipe and a money-bag. You may find a Nelson, a Napoleon, a Frederick the Great, a Lord Howe or the famous Duke of York,

> Who had 10,000 men
> And when he'd marched them up the hill
> He marched them down again.

Nor does this exhaust the list. There is even a female Toby called "Woman" in brown ware; also "Toby's Wife", 10 inches high and showing a seated female in a mob cap. One of these women is Martha Gunn, the Brighton bathing-woman who taught George the Third to swim as a child. She has the Prince of Wales feathers in her hat. There are also miniatures of Tobies. All have a great variety of colour. In fact, one of the charms of Toby is his almost inexhaustible variety. He is a great favourite in the United States. No wonder the genuine variety of Toby gets rarer and costlier as time passes.

In a Toby with a lid (which usually sends up the price), the lid is generally his hat. That also forms a cup-like vessel for drinking from. Of course, the idea is to pour the contents of the jug into the hat, each hatful being a drink a a time.

You may also find Toby tea-pots, mustard-pots, pepper-casters, inkpots and mugs, but they are often counterfeits. Since there are so many modern imitations it may be well to learn how to tell the real from the sham right at the beginning. If there is a signature, that helps, but many fine specimens are unsigned.

The great potters who first made the Toby jugs—men

like Whieldon, the two Ralph Woods, Voyez, Walton, Hollins or Neale—knew secrets other craftsmen did not. By long experience and great skill they knew which colours would "stand the fire" in baking the clay and emerge shining and beautiful. That brings me to the test of the real, old *versus* the sham and modern. As in so much of antique judgment, you must train your eye to look carefully. In the shams, the colour is crude, dirty-looking, smudgily put on. It is not good colour with richness or depth in it. Take your handkerchief, wet it, and rub the colour. In some forgeries the work is so badly scamped that the colours will come off upon your moistened handkerchief. This shows that the faker has not troubled to "fire" the Toby after painting. (Not all imitations, however, are as bad as this.)

Next look for marks of genuine wear and tear on your Toby, such as chips or abrasions. Remember, however, that in good "fakes" these can be counterfeited by skilful filing or a piece of emery paper. Good tests of old age are discoloration and iridescence, the latter being the more reliable. Forgers have been known to let beer "simmer" in the jug for a long time to produce discoloration. This iridescence—rainbow colours darkened by the under hues— is a special feature of Whieldon ware and old Rockingham pottery. Do not mistake this for "crazing" or cracking of the glaze easily visible and very common. That is due not to the age with its slow action of air and light, but to bad "firing", which is rapid. It is easy for the forger to "craze" his products and to rub ochre into them to intensify the aged appearance. Colour-quality and iridescence are therefore the best and most reliable tests—which applies to other pottery as well.

An esteemed kind of eighteenth-century jug is a Pratt jug. Felix Pratt worked from about 1780 to 1820. His jugs vary in height from 4 to 8 inches; the usual colours are orange-yellow and a purplish shade with green and blue and brown. Pratt jugs, and indeed all Pratt work, including his mugs, plates, tea-pots, flasks and figures, are vigorous in style and highly distinctive. Often the decoration consists of vine-leaves or acanthus. The jugs show sporting subjects like a hare and hounds and huntsmen, or celebrities of the period such as Lord Nelson.

It may interest you to know that one of the greatest authorities today on Toby jugs is the Chairman of the National Savings Movement, Lord Mackintosh. In one of his articles he tells of an invoice dated 1783 from Ralph Wood to the great Josiah Wedgwood (the first) for 300 Toby jugs, the pieces being priced between only two shillings and a few pence, the total amount being for £9 6s. 4d. Lord Mackintosh calculates that the value of those 300 today would be over £20,000. That gives you some idea of how antiques can appreciate over the years.

On one Toby by the elder Ralph Wood, marked "R.W." and 1770, appears the following distich:

> *No art with potters' can compare:*
> *We make our jugs of what we potters are.*

There is a great truth enshrined in this last line. We are apt to forget that the jugs are not merely made of clay and pigments but of the maker's character, knowledge and experience in life. The creative artist cannot avoid putting himself and his soul into his work—and the greater the man the greater the work.

*   *   *

If everybody has seen a Toby jug, everybody has not only seen but also heard of Wedgwood pottery. It is distinctive in its classicism and utterly unlike anything else. Josiah Wedgwood has a good claim to be considered the greatest English potter and is ranked even with Della Robbia and Palissy. The firm of Wedgwood is still turning out artistic products today. "Wedgwood" is the chief glory of English earthenware.

Amateurs often think that any bit of Wedgwood is immensely valuable, but it is *old* Wedgwood and its finest pieces which make large sums. Old Wedgwood is still to be picked up by the zealous hunter after it.

How is the beginner to distinguish between old and modern Wedgwood which, at a glance, look so much alike?

First there is the mark. The main mark is the name "Wedgwood" impressed in the paste before it is fired. The size of the letters varies from $\frac{1}{4}$ to $\frac{1}{32}$ of an inch in height. Occasionally only the first letter "W" is a capital letter.

For a time Wedgwood was in partnership with Bentley, and during that period the names were conjoined thus: WEDGWOOD & BENTLEY. One early partnership mark consists of the two names in a circle. In some later ones the word ETRURIA is added with an inner and an outer ring. Etruria was the name of his factory, but had to be given up as a mark, as foreign buyers did not understand it.

The mark JOSIAH WEDGWOOD with a date underneath (such as Feb. 3. 1805) belongs to the time when the business was carried on by the son of the original founder. If Wedgwood is misspelt Wedgewood you may be sure the piece does not belong to the Etruria works.

From 1891 onward the word "England" has been always added to Wedgwood.

The main mark is not the only mark. There are also date marks. Three arbitrary letters are stamped on each piece in close promixity. The first two letters used to represent the private mark of the individual potter and the third letter the year. Again and again the alphabet was gone through. Some years ago, the firm recognised that this method of marking the date was imperfect. For instance, a letter "J" might mean the year 1855, or 1881, or 1907. So they altered the date-letter to a figure.

This makes deciphering the date from the marks difficult for beginners unless they have a key. If you write to the firm in Staffordshire they will help, and the Wedgwood Society of London, whose Honorary Secretary is Mr. des Fontayne, issues a most useful list of old Wedgwood dates and marks from 1730 to 1820.

The collector needs to distinguish between "Old Wedgwood" and "Wedgwood Ware". By the "ware" old Josiah Wedgwood wrote that he meant "such vessels as are made use of at meals". Of his medallions (which he called his "tablets") he wrote: "They are not the ware."

Now "Old Wedgwood" is the original Wedgwood work in jasper and basalt earthenware. This is rare and costly. The black basalt is much less valuable than the jasper. Besides Wedgwood there is good jasper ware made by Adams and Turner and others. If less rare and costly than the other, "Wedgwood ware" is certainly worth collecting as being of real and increasing value. Wedgwood ware is that excellent cream-coloured, plainly pencilled or transfer-printed neat pottery made for the table. It is always graceful, often beautiful. Invariably it is suitable for its purpose.

So widespread was the fame of Old Wedgwood that to this day it can be picked up in France, Italy, Germany, Holland and other European countries. The first Wedgwood had agents in Paris and other continental cities. Both his useful and ornamental pieces were sold abroad on an extensive scale. It is pleasant to find that Wedgwood-hunting can be done by the amateur on a continental holiday just as well as when he is at home in England.

"Old Wedgwood" has more than its marks to identify

it. It should be taken as a general rule in the acquisition of antiques never to rely upon the marks alone. The piece, whatever it be, should be brought to the test of quality and style. Marks can be imitated and may be forgeries. This warning should never be forgotten.

One good test of intrinsic quality in judging Old Wedgwood is the feel of the surface. It has been compared to the softness and smoothness of a baby's skin. Sir Arthur Church, a great authority on the subject, compared it with ivory and said it is neither "dry and chalky looking on the one hand nor of waxy smoothness on the other". The late Sir James Yoxall, a great connoisseur and my old friend and mentor, described it as feeling to the fingers "like a clay-pipe which has a film of soap-bubble over it—just the least bit soapy and almost wet". Verbal descriptions, helpful though they may be, are less useful than touch. Once you have felt the surface—preferably several times—you are likely to know and unlikely to be deceived. Nothing can compare with actual experience—the sight and touch of oneself applied to the object again and again—for training the beginner.

Some ten years after the first Josiah Wedgwood's death in 1795, defects began to occur in Wedgwood: bubbles and holes and ripples and stringiness appeared. In the "old" there are no such flaws. On the contrary, the uniformity of grain and surface giving an almost satin-like feeling to the fingers is obvious.

What inspired Wedgwood to some of his finest works was Grecian art. He laboured for years to produce the ideal medium in which to make plaques, cameos, vases and similar ornamental forms. Not till about 1770 did he find that barium sulphate from Derbyshire used as an ingredient, resulted in his famous "jasper" ware. This jasper needs no description. The pieces on a lavender-blue ground relieved by raised busts or other figures in pure white are familiar to almost everybody. They are notable for delicate colouring and charming effects. Other colours besides the very familiar blue were used. Reliefs were designed by famous artists like John Flaxman or Wedgwood's own designer Hackwood; or they were copied from ancient cameos, intaglios or coins of ancient Greece or Rome.

Wedgwood's most famous piece was his copy of the "Portland Vase" of the ancients, named after the Duke of Portland who lent him the vase for copying. He made fifty copies in blue-black jasper with white reliefs and asked 50 guineas each for them. One of his copies is worth four figures today—if you can find such a treasure.

As you will well understand, the success of Wedgwood the First very quickly attracted rivals and competitors in his native Staffordshire, other parts of England and also abroad. The Woods—the two Ralphs and Enoch—famous for their figures, began successfully to make cream-ware, black basalt and jasper. Jasper by Adams of Tunstall is rated as beautiful as Wedgwood. The famous Spode was another rival. There was much borrowing and imitation.

One cannot ignore another achievement of Wedgwood's. His perfecting of the cream-coloured ware which, out of compliment to George the Third's Queen Charlotte, he named "Queen's Ware". It was light, durable and very finely made and became an instant success which it deserved. Pieces of it dating from the 1760's may still be found. Once again they have been much copied.

There are innumerable varieties of old English earthenware. It is impossible to list and describe them all here. Books have been written and will continue to be written on this almost inexhaustible subject. Many varieties of ware are not likely to be found by the beginner. Some would be of little interest to him even if they were located.

However, it may be useful to indicate to the beginner the principal types desirable to collect:

1. The first is "slipware" of the seventeenth century. "Slip" was a creamy liquid made of clay diffused in water. It was used to decorate, often being marked over the whole or part of the surface. Wrotham slipware has a red body ornamented with white slip in heavy patches. It is usually stamped with masks, fleurs-de-lys, rosettes and crosses, surrounded by radiating borders on the rim. Toft slipware, light, buff or red body with white or yellow body, is famous and much sought after.

Slipware—of which Wrotham and Toft are the two main classes—has been described by Mr. Honey, one of the very greatest authorities on the subject, as "some of the most distinctive of all English pottery". Wrotham goes from the year 1612 to the 1720's. Toft dates from 1670.

2. Then there is Delftware, of which Adam and Eve dishes of the seventeenth century are the famous samples. These are generally large dishes. Adam and Eve are really King William III and Mary his Queen. The apple tree bears oranges instead of apples since William was "of Orange". These dishes are known as "chargers". (You may remember that in the Bible, Salome, the daughter of Herodias, asked King Herod for the head of John the Baptist "on a charger", i.e. a dish.) As there are often blue dashes on the rims, these specimens are known as "Blue-Dash Chargers".

If you wish to study Delftware in detail the best book for your purpose is *English Delftware*, by Professor F. H. Garner (1948).

3. Stoneware. This pottery was fired at a very high temperature which gave it a peculiar hardness and it is usually coated with a thin glaze. Three types are recognised as famous for excellence: (1) Dwight's stoneware made at Fulham, (2) stoneware made at Nottingham (often jugs

80

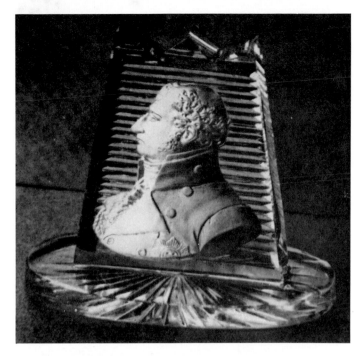

Three types of paperweight: *above*, a cut-glass portrait of Frederick, Duke of York, etched against a background of deep, horizontal cutting. *Bottom*, George III (*left*) and George IV (*right*) on cross-cut diamond background

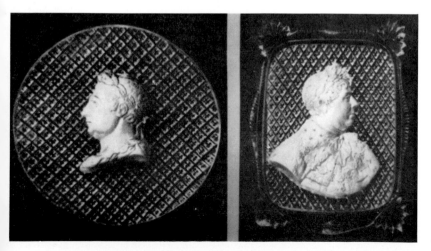

Scent bottle with portrait of George IV

An early nineteenth-century French gold-and-enamel snuff-box, made by L. A. Ricart

in the shape of a bear and pitchers), and Staffordshire
stoneware associated with the name of Elers.

John Dwight, an Oxford graduate and a patentee of
King Charles II, was a very remarkable man. Artistically
the statuettes made at the Dwight factory are exceptionally
fine. They are also very rare, each having been a separate
work. Sir Arthur Church describes them as "a brilliant out-
burst of the potter's genius" and as "triumphs" of the art.

James Morley of Nottingham made stoneware resembling
Dwight's, but the colours are various shades of brown.
Nottingham brown stoneware is often dated as between
1700 and 1800, but Dwight is older, ranging from about
1670.

John and David Elers are responsible for red-coloured
stoneware. Their style is very fine and thin. Great skill and
charm are shown in Elers' ware, especially in the delicate
red tea-pots which are very famous.

4. Later improvements led to a new type of pottery known
as Salt-glaze. It is much sought after and very valuable. It
is a white or light-coloured stoneware after the Dwight
kind, but characterised by a minute pitting such as may be
seen on orange peel or fine leather. Its name comes from
the fact that the glaze is calcined salt. It may be studied, as
it deserves to be, in collections at the British Museum and
the South Kensington Museum, also in others throughout
the land—especially at Hanley, Cambridge and Manchester.

The taking of Portobello was a favourite subject in the
year 1739 and long after. The "Portobello" pieces are
especially famous. Figures are rare, but there are small
animals. In addition there are what are called "Pew-groups"
—little tiny dolls with crinkled hair sitting in pews. These
pew-groups have been imitated, but other fakes in salt-
glaze are not common. However, you may know the true
from the false by the orange peel, or fine leather, pitting

already alluded to; also by what has been described as "the exquisite half-gloss" of the true variety.

5. Earthenware Statuettes, Astbury-Whieldon ware. The chimney ornament figures made by the Woods, Whieldon, Walton and other Staffordshire potters 150 or so years ago depend for their value on marks identifying them, upon the artistry of their modelling, or both—so both points should be regarded. There is doubt whether this lovely pottery should be ascribed to John Astbury and his son Thomas or to Thomas Whieldon—hence the double-barrelled name now generally attached to it. For the beginner the name is of little consequence. What he needs to do is to study this class, like the others, at first hand; learn to recognise it at sight, corroborating his recognition by the evidence of marks, if these exist.

6. Leeds Ware. This should be especially looked for as there is a good chance for the amateur here. It is a cream-ware which the firm of Hartley Greens and Company began to produce at Leeds about 1783. Apart from its great merit and market value, it is a particularly good field. Many small dealers know very little about it and think all "Leeds" must be lace-like and pierced ware. This is not correct; but many dealers believe it, so are apt to undervalue other "Leeds" which they acquire. Also they are apt to think its mugs and jugs must have double-twisted handles to be genuine "Leeds". This is a mistake.

The wideawake amateur going antique-hunting therefore may pick up bargains in "Leeds" ware. How is he to identify it? Unfortunately in some cases the marks of Leeds, or the name "Leeds" and even "Leeds Pottery" and the name of "Hartley Greens & Co." have been copied rather often on other wares. Further identification may be necessary. Extremely light weight and especial fineness of glaze are far safer guides.

The light weight of "Leeds" is one of its chief characteristics. The cream fine glaze has a decidedly visible tinge of green about it—a faintly yellowish, not bluish, green. Usually this glaze is very little scratched and seldom crazed. The tone of the whole is "that smooth rich cream colour" —with the hint of green about it.

7. Willow-pattern earthenware. Because everyone has seen this familiar design, the most common of all patterns, it is not to be despised when it is early work. Thomas Minton is said to have invented the pattern at Caughley. What is certain is that it "caught on" and soon scores of potters were imitating it. The early, not the later work, is worth the collector's attention.

The earlier work is in shades of cobalt, but sometimes in black. Then it is usually Wedgwood's work. Printing in reds, purples or browns is chiefly Victorian (i.e. relatively late). These colours never appealed to buyers so well as the blues did.

In the original Minton the pagoda is put on the right-hand side and there are 32 apples on the tallest tree. Leeds ware shows 63 apples; Swansea 30. Willow-pattern work by Spode has 32; Copeland 31; the Clews 34; and Wedgwood 34. You perceive that you must take the trouble to observe the numerous and interesting varieties of this immortal pattern—of which the number of apples is only one distinctive feature.

The number of people shown walking on the bridge also may vary. It can either be two or three men. The first holds a crook, the second a roll of paper, the third a lantern. Often the fence is differently rendered. On Spode it may be a swastika. There are also particular patterns on the rim of a plate. By a study of these details you may learn to identify willow-pattern work of Leeds, Swansea and Rockingham as well as of individual potters such as Clews, Turner and Adams.

The Chinese legend which this pattern seems to commemorate is the tale of an errant daughter who eloped with her lover. Her father pursues the fleeing couple. Arriving at a stream they take refuge in a boat and sail away. The irate parent catches and slays both of them, whereupon their faithful souls turn into the twin-doves depicted in the sky. This story, illustrated on many thousands of plates, fascinated and delighted many generations of English children at meal-times.

For the amateur the important thing is knowing how to distinguish between the later and the earlier work. Useful points are the colour of the body of the plate, the shade of the blue, the slight rippling in the earlier glaze and the way in which the engraving is done. The modern work has a brighter glaze, a colder blue, and a harder design. There is a softness about the earlier work quite absent from the later specimens.

As to the way in which the engraving is done: the line-engraving of the earlier work is finer than the "stippling" in dots introduced later. The earthenware itself has a creamy tinge compared with the white (very clean-looking) of Victorian and later examples. Then of course there may be marks to help. Spode, for example, is usually marked and so are Wedgwood, Copeland and Davenport. Many makes carry no name and one can only go by the appearance in distinguishing the old from the new.

If you do not wish to collect willow-pattern ware in quantity, you may still like one or two pieces as ornaments. For example, a plate hung on a wall can be very decorative, and there are pieces still more ornamental. For a few shillings I picked up a lidded circular box shaped like a miniature jam-jar nearly 3 inches high. The dealer who sold it told me he had no idea what it was and he thought it was modern. "Too pretty to be old", he thought. On scouring it I found on the base the name Wedgwood clearly impressed with four dots beneath and at an angle the figure "7". From its "soft" appearance I guessed it was early work. Submitting it to a Wedgwood expert, he had no doubt that the date was about 1840, and the value several times what I gave.

Even if one is not a collector of willow-pattern, such a piece as this lends distinction and beauty wherever it is placed and can be put in almost any room in the house. Furthermore, it can be used as a container—the least of its virtues—but one not to be ignored by those who like household pieces to be useful as well as ornamental.

9

Old English China

Now for china and porcelain, which subject follows naturally upon pottery and earthenware, being obviously related.

Make no mistake at the beginning. The study of china and porcelain—the two terms, though often interchanged, are *not* precisely synonymous—is a huge undertaking. Oriental and continental porcelains are vast and expensive subjects in themselves. The amateur may be content to confine his early efforts to the mastery of the main facts regarding Old English China. He will find that quite difficult and absorbing enough.

English China, often called bone china, is not, technically, true porcelain because of the ingredient of bone-ash in its composition which produces a "soft" paste as against the "hard" paste which is porcelain. The great Professor Church calls Old English China "an ingenuous and beautiful counterfeit of the ware it purposed to reproduce". Briefly, then, it is an imitation of Chinese ware which the English potters made with substitutes for the oriental ingredients. On the other hand, old Dresden is a true porcelain and not a bone china.

This distinction, having been grasped as it should be, right at the beginning, one comes to what the impatient beginner always wants to know. He has heard of Chelsea, of Bow, of Worcester and of Derby and asks: "How can I quickly and easily distinguish between these various makes? I want to be able to say whether a piece is one, or any of the others.

Or, if it is none of them, then a miserable fake with which I should have no concern."

Probably he thinks this little enough to ask. He expects what he would call "a straight answer" to his very reasonable and sensible question. Unfortunately it is not so easy or simple as that—far from it. The knowledge sought is essentially practical knowledge as distinct from book expositions of it. Books can help, but, as I have said before, the vital knowledge must be gained at first hand by sight and touch in museums, auction-rooms, antique-shops, and market-places. There is no substitute for this practical experience where china and porcelain are concerned.

You are surprised, perhaps, because you have heard of "marks" and at least of the famous Chelsea "anchor". Alas! Chelsea is sometimes forged. Or if Chelsea at all, then it may be a modern reproduction of the old. Also, a large proportion of the old china is unmarked. Sad to relate, even contemporaries copied and also forged the marks. You may quite easily master half a dozen or more of the principal English marks, but remember that the classic English text-book is a thick stout volume, called *Chaffers Marks on English Pottery and China*. So marks, useful though they be, may mislead in some cases and are by no means the whole story in identification.

Fortunately for the beginner's peace of mind, the study of Old English China is a short one since it covers a brief space of time. The exact date is unknown, but roughly speaking English china started about the year 1750. Pottery, as you already know, is very much older than that. China after 1850 or so is not reckoned as "Old English China". Some fastidious collectors would reject any pieces made later than 1800 or at most, 1825. It was the making of old Dresden and old Sévres in Germany and France that started the English factories on Old English China, often inaccurately called old English porcelain. There were only about nineteen or twenty important factories and some of them quickly came to grief. Dates are dubious. Chelsea, Bow, Longton Hall and Derby started about 1760, Worcester in 1751, Liverpool and Lowestoft a few years later. Plymouth, Bristol, New Hall and Caughley started about 1770. These eleven form the earliest lot.

(Later on Caughley was absorbed by the Coalport factory, also known as Colebrookdale, about 1800.)

A second group of makers was Coalport, Pinxton, Nantgarw, Swansea, Spode, Minton, Davenport and Rockingham. These are regarded as being 1800 or later. Pinxton and the Welsh makers did not last long, but Rockingham did for about twenty years.

In general Plymouth and Bristol are distinguished by making a "hard paste". New Hall, in a class by itself, is sometimes hard, sometimes soft. The remainder made a soft paste. This difference is to be noted for purposes of identification.

To the connoisseur, Old English China primarily means Bow, Chelsea, early Worcester, early Derby, Langton Hall, Liverpool, Caughley, Lowestoft, Plymouth, Bristol and early New Hall. In a word, eighteenth-century ware, but the nineteenth century also has its adherents and its products have decided attractions.

With this background of essential knowledge, the beginner is in a position to learn what he wants, and needs to know, above all else: namely, how to identify the various makes and distinguish the real antique from the false imitation. Remember that, while helpful, the mark, if it exists, is not sufficient. You need other criteria.

Many authorities say that the first step is to learn to tell "soft" paste from hard. This is good advice but limited. Some fine antique porcelains, such as Bristol, are hard and

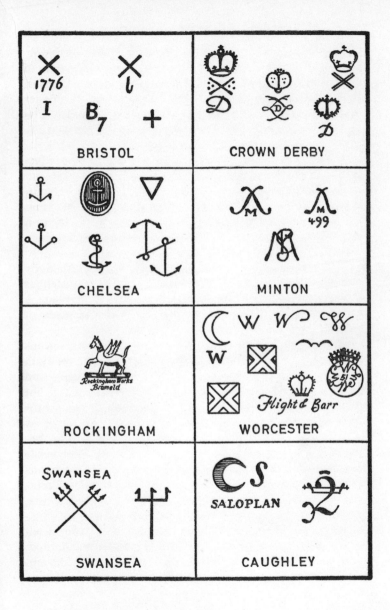

BRISTOL

CROWN DERBY

CHELSEA

MINTON

ROCKINGHAM

WORCESTER

SWANSEA

CAUGHLEY

of course a mere imitation also would be hard. Nevertheless, when dealing with "soft" antiques, fakes will be found to be hard. To distinguish this difference in kind is important. How can the beginner do it?

If you smash the china you could tell instantly, but who wants to break valuable china, rendering it neither valuable nor china, in order to find out of what it is made? What a broken piece would reveal in a second is this. The edges, if "hard" paste, would be quite smooth; the edge of "soft" paste, however, relatively rough.

Breakage being out of the question, what is the alternative test? Take your piece (or whatever the object is) and search its back or bottom for any small space (which may perhaps be on the rim) where the glaze has missed covering the body-space of the object. Pass your fingernail over the spot. If it feels hard and gritty that speaks for itself as hard-paste china. On the other hand, if it has a "soapy" feel, it is soft-paste china. Another test is to use a small steel file where it will show the least and do the minimum damage. It will mark the soft, but not the hard, china. No, not even a scratch. You may shrink from using the file on fine specimens—so another test is to look carefully at the glaze. It has a very different appearance on the two kinds. On the soft, the glaze seems to be a part of the paste as if it had sunk in: this is because the soft is porous and absorbent. The glaze on the hard does not appear to have sunk in but to be on the surface. Finally there is the test of touch. As compared with the soft, the hard feels cold to the touch.

You perceive now that if the amateur will take a little trouble in first learning these simple practical tests and then apply them, he can quite easily master the expert knowledge of identifying Old English China so far as its composition is concerned. To change the beginner into the expert all that is required is first-hand experience of looking at, and handling, china.

Useful as this is, it does not enable one to say with confidence of any given piece: "This is Bow" or "That is Derby" or "This is certainly Chelsea". Here books, photographs and other illustrations can be of the greatest help. Unfortunately simplicity disappears and complexity enters. Broadly speaking, several factories took their ideas of design and decoration from the same sources and copied each other quite shamelessly.

You have to make a study of the type of china made by the famous school or schools that interest you. You must look at the paste, the glaze, the shape, the modelling, the style, the painting and so forth. Finally you look at the piece as a whole, recognise the individual impression which it creates and the total result should give you the answer: "This is typical ware of Bow or Chelsea" or whatever else it might be.

There will be instances so free from doubt that even a complete beginner will be able to identify with confidence. We are, of course, talking about a very distinctive piece. However, in many cases, even an expert may be uncertain, and need to make the most careful, detailed, painstaking examination before giving an opinion. Here is a lovely little figure. At once the expert says "either Chelsea or Bow". Before he can decide precisely which with certainty, he may have to consult his books, then look into the subtlest differences.

Detection can be very difficult. To many collectors, that is part of the fun of the game. Let me illustrate the point. This plate, for example, looks like Worcester. Remembering that Caughley copied the Worcester designs and even used their mark, one must be cautious in proclaiming the plate Worcester. Both are about the same date. Indeed, you might have two lovely plates looking exactly alike, yet one will be Worcester, the other Caughley. Difficult as this is, in this particular case there is a simple test which not only the expert, but the greenhorn, can use to solve the problem immediately. Apply a strong light behind the plate. If it is Worcester, the paste of the plate will show a greenish tinge; if it is Caughley it shows a brownish hue.

The fact must be faced that even the connoisseur of wide reading and many years' experience of china and porcelain sometimes comes across baffling cases. Coalport's copies of Chelsea or Worcester are instances in point. Then there is Longton Hall. On first impression it might be Liverpool, Bow or early Derby. More than ordinary knowledge is needed here. The only prudent course for the beginner here is to seek expert advice—from museums and dealers. When in doubt, refrain from acquisition. Fortunately such skilled advice is readily available and generally free.

Another thing may add to the difficulties of the novice. In the case of nineteenth-century English china, a standardised paste began to be used. (Much of this particular china, however, is marked plainly.) Therefore it is not always possible to distinguish one variety from another by paste.

All these difficulties fade, though they do not vanish, when the beginner starts gaining practical experience. With the actual china before us, and with very little knowledge indeed, we should recognise what the china before us actually is. We can be pretty certain. Here we see the yellowish tone of early Bow, there the greyish colour of Liverpool ware, or the cold, almost snowy white, of hard Bristol, heavy-looking paste of Longton Hall, the bluey glaze of Lowestoft, and finally the glassy-looking paste of Nantgarw. Then just look at the distinctive colours: that purple and emerald-green of Bow, the browny-red of Lowestoft, the yellowy-green of Longton Hall, and deep blue of

Worcester. Soon you have a picture fixed in your mind's eye of what may be expected in any one of the famous early English chinas.

Practical experience—looking, comparing, handling—is everything. Book-knowledge cannot replace practical observation and the experience that brings this book-knowledge and the illustrations to life. Fortunately practical experience of the quest for fine examples of Old English China costs nothing. It is perennially interesting and attractive both to the eager beginner and the seasoned collector. One more word of caution, and it applies in this field rather than some others. Do not purchase until you have gained rudimentary knowledge of the kind of china you are tempted to buy.

Finally, let me add this. The beginner may be fascinated at the outset by continental porcelain and dazzled by exquisite examples of old Dresden or Sèvres—the aristocracy of ceramics. Since such purchases are very expensive, quite beyond the purses of most of us, the amateur should wait before indulging in this kind of luxury. At least until he has learned so much about ceramics as to be no longer an amateur. A course in Old English China is excellent groundwork for more daring adventures in collecting. If you wish to study Sèvres, the best places to do so are the Wallace Collection at Hertford House, Manchester Square, and the splendid collection of the Bowes Museum at Barnard Castle.

10

Old English Glass (1)

WHAT strictly is meant by the term Old English Glass?

To the historian it is a lengthy study extending from the days of Ancient Rome's invasion of Great Britain; to the collector and antique-lover it is a very short period indeed, starting at earliest in the reign of Charles II—say about 1680—and lasting at the latest until about 1820. The above definition excludes even Victorian glass, however good, clear, and however finely cut, but some collectors wisely collect Victorian almost as avidly as Georgian pieces.

Nor is it only "period" that defines old English glass in the collectors' sense. Bowls, beakers, dishes and platters, lamps, bottles and jars of all kinds in glass are to be found from the time of the Roman occupation. The mass of collectors take little, if any, interest in all these articles. What they collect is drinking-glasses for wine, spirits, cordials, ales, also jugs, decanters, salt-cellars and so on, usually found in cut-glass. In this connection the term "drinking-glasses" includes sweetmeat-glasses. As a general rule, collectors place most emphasis upon the drinking-glasses, and many collectors confine their attention solely to them.

Beginners will do well to follow this trend, although they will certainly be tempted to include a few Georgian decanters amongst their treasures. It has been said that nine out of every ten glass-collectors who are amateurs of old English glass concern themselves solely with drinking-glasses and so forth, dating from the eighteenth century.

Therefore the historical side of English glass may be dealt with very briefly here and only in so far as it is helpful to the amateur collector to have a general background picture. Everyone has heard of the Portland Vase which, as we have seen, was finely copied by Wedgwood and, after being smashed by a lunatic, is now repaired and back in the British Museum. That magnificent vase, a triumph in cutting, colour and design was made of glass by some ancient Roman for a wealthy client. There also was glass in Egypt and Syria 3,000 years ago. After the Romans, the Moslems made glass and wonderful old specimens exist in old mosques. Following the Moslems, the next advance was with the Venetians whose coloured and crystalline glass taught Europe—and especially Bohemia—what "cristalls" could achieve in beauty and fitness. Venetian glass-makers came to England in the time of Queen Elizabeth the First. Their most famous name is Jacob Verzeline. A very few "museum pieces" of his survive to this day.

In the British Museum collection there is a fine drinking-glass or goblet made by Verzeline bearing the date 1586 and the motto: "In God is all my Trust." Following Verzeline, monopolies in glass-making were granted to various successors, including Admiral Sir Richard Mansel who dominated English glass-making for forty years.

The Civil War stopped all fine glass-manufacture. In the Restoration period, with a charter from King Charles the Company of London Glass-Sellers went ahead. Their man, George Ravenscroft, experimented boldly, especially by adding lead-oxide to the basic silica. He succeeded partly by creating a new type of glass—the famous "lead crystal". So English glass, as known to the antique-collector, began.

Very few Ravenscroft glasses survive. Naturally they fetch extremely high prices. The beginner need not trouble himself further about them, for it is extremely unlikely that he will ever find any, except in some famous collection. The point is that Ravenscroft's discovery was a revolution in English glass-technique; it created that eighteenth-century glass which is what collectors usually mean when they talk of "old English glass". It should be said that this new lead-glass was not only more durable but superior to its ancestral Venetian and Bohemian glass by reason of its lustrous depth. From its inception it was fashionable and a great commercial success.

You have probably heard of Irish glass by the esteemed names of "Waterford glass" and "Cork glass". It is less probable that you will have heard of Scottish glass. Both Scottish and Irish glass are generally included under the specification of "Old English", but owing to its intrinsic excellence and fame Irish glass requires separate attention later in this chapter.

So much for the historic background of glass necessary for the beginner to know, put as clearly and briefly as possible. It will be observed that this is written merely from the collector's standpoint and takes no account—for example—of stained window-glasses, a study of its own.

Those who wish, later on, to study the story of glass in its wider aspect and in more detail are referred to such authorities as *English Glass*, by W. B. Harley (Collins), of the Victoria and Albert Museum, or another book of the same name by W. A. Thorpe of the same museum. There is also *Irish Glass*, by M. S. Dudley Westropp (Herbert Jenkins), and a good cheap book is *Glass*, by E. Barrington Haynes (in the Pelican series). For practical purposes and for those with light purses, the last book may be sufficient, especially as its special section on drinking-glasses illustrates all the main types and shapes of bowl, foot, stem and general structure.

[Photo: Delieb Antiques Ltd.]

A selection of vinaigrettes

Staffordshire Toby jug, $10\frac{1}{2}$ inches high and coloured blue and white

Minton porcelain vase, made in 1867

Portland vase by Josiah Wedgwood, made in 1793

However, I do not advise the beginner to start with these books for one very good reason. (Indeed, I advise *against* them at first.) The wealth of detail inevitable in a complete account of this subject—admirable and desirable as it is for the advanced student and the seasoned expert—can only bewilder and confuse the beginner. Its complexity may easily dishearten and discourage him, or her, in an early stage, whereas later in his progress he may find it stimulating. After the beginner has mastered what is said in this book he may then move on to more profound works.

Even at this stage it must become plain that the large number of shapes and varieties of drinking-glasses of the eighteenth century (leaving out altogether Victorian glass) presents a formidable study. Worse, new varieties turn up from time to time to surprise dealers and collectors. (By "new", I mean new in detail, not in their basic type.) A book which illustrates this fact well is what used to be, and to some degree still is, the classic and standard work on English glasses written by Albert Hartshorne in 1897. If you can borrow that from a library, and compare it with one of the more modern books, you will see that largely because of new finds, this great work has become out of date in some respects.

In old English glass as defined for collecting-purposes, there are three broad classes: namely, English, Scottish or Irish glass generally; next, the coloured or opaque glass usually attributed to Bristol; and finally, the type associated with the word Nailsea, which most educated people know by its being enamelled in white loops or coloured stripes.

Now "Bristol" and "Nailsea" have special attractions for some collectors. It is easy to understand that, for they are not unattractive in themselves. However, they are not the main or usual interest of glass-collectors in general. For this reason, also because there is much modern imitation of Bristol and Nailsea, they will be dealt with later in the chapter upon "Trifles and Curiosities".

Turning then to British and Irish glass specifically, a point needs to be noted about Irish glass. It used to be positively asserted that Irish glass could be distinguished from English by tints in the glass. People said that Waterford glass had a bluish tinge and Cork glass a yellowish from which English glass was reputedly free. This belief had considerable currency for about fifty years. Then a great expert in the National Museum at Dublin, Mr. Westropp, showed that Irish was usually as "white" as English and that some English had either the blue, or the yellow, tint. Still even now, glass with that bluish tint is greatly prized and often sold as "Waterford" at a high price. While this may be right in some, perhaps many, cases, all blue-tint glass is not necessarily Irish.

Some Irish glass—unlike most glass—is marked: as, for example, "Penrose, Waterford". Where this is so, that of course speaks for itself. Irish design too is often distinctive. Mark and design are more reliable than "blue tint", but the "blue tint", while not conclusive, is not altogether to be despised as a frequent characteristic, helpful to the judgment.

Now the beginner wants, so far as possible, a clear picture as a guide to sorting out the various styles. Let us see how this may be given to him.

First take the bowl and its shape. It may be shaped like a funnel, or a bell, or waisted, or so on. Unfortunately the shapes—familiar to us all from cheap reproductions—are not confined to definite periods. They help very little, if at all, in dating specimens, since they were used throughout the eighteenth century—and indeed to this very day.

Next take the foot of an antique drinking-glass. What has been said of the bowl is true of the foot inasmuch as the various forms of it do not help in dating. The foot is noticeably wide compared with the modern; sometimes it has a folded edge or is very much "domed". Neither of these points *alone* determines any date, though they may be taken into account with other points of style. What does really help is the stem of the glass. This is easily the most significant feature. It often enables the approximate date of the glass to be judged and also assists the classification.

Now what points about the stem are to be noted? The stems of drinking-glasses of the eighteenth century (which we are considering as desirable to find and collect) fall into four groups: the Baluster, *circa* (that is: about) 1711, the Silesian, 1725, the Drawn-Stem and Straight-Stem, *circa* 1750, and lastly the Cut-Stem to the end of the century. Let us look at each one of these in some detail.

The "Baluster" type of stem is found on the earliest eighteenth-century glasses and so called because of the swellings or "knops" on it. These suggest the idea of a small balustrade. These "knops" can be of various shapes and sizes. Some glasses have one "knop" only and occasionally there is a coin of Queen Anne, or a bubble of air (called a tear) in them. As a rule the larger and heavier-looking the "knops", the earlier will be the glass. Specially tall and graceful glasses with a lighter baluster stem are usually known as "Newcastle glasses". So much for the baluster.

The second type, the Silesian, came into fashion just before the first King George ascended the throne. This stem is a moulded pedestal. It has broad shoulders and tapers down towards the foot with rounded ribs dividing it. The most usual form is octagonal. There is sometimes one "knop" above the pedestal. Not only drinking-glasses but glass candlesticks of this period often had Silesian stems. The style is commonest with champagne and sweet-meat glasses. It had a long life, lasting for some forty years.

The third type of stem was a straight, slim one, much thinner than the two preceding kinds. It may be plain with no decoration, or decorated by a tear or with spiral twists. The new style was caused not merely by a contemporary change of fashion, as you might suppose. What happened was that the Excise Act 1745-6 taxed glass-ingredients by weight so that economy in weight became important to the glaziers and makers. Less lead—for lead of course is a very heavy metal—was used, and designs were made lighter.

There were several varieties of twist: the air-spirals, the opaque-white, the coloured and mixed, spirals. Long elaborate explanations of the skilled processes by which these were produced can be found in the larger text-books, and it would be foreign to our purpose to enlarge upon them here. Knowledge of how glasses are made is technical and does not assist the amateur either to date or to differentiate them.

The fourth group of cut stems belongs to the latter part of the eighteenth century and lasted until its end—or a little after. These are most beautiful stems with shallow facets—either dome-shaped or six-sided; they may be either straight or "knopped". Cut glass in general will be dealt with in a later chapter.

It must not be thought from the precision with which the divisions into Baluster, Silesian, Straight and Cut have been set out that there is always a clean-cut total difference in all the actual specimens of each sort. There may be a feature or two normally associated with one group found in another or in several. For instance, a baluster may have an air-twist though usually it does not. So too a cut stem may have a "knop". While accurate as far as it goes, the dating is imprecise as has been indicated by the use of the word "*circa*"; yet the grouping is of real help in dating. It is a guide to know approximately, since exactitude is impossible, when each basic style came in, how long it remained the fashion, and when it was superseded by the new type.

Precision in dating, as we know it in antique or modern silver and gold, for instance, is impossible with old English glass.

A familiar and popular form of glass recognised by people outside the ranks of collectors by name and appearance is known as a "Rummer". It was an old public-house glass used as the name shows for rum. The rummer is a distinct glass because of its extremely short or almost non-existent stem. This class includes some wine and ale glasses with short sturdy stems, some dwarf ale-glasses and some jelly glasses. If eighteenth century, they date probably from its last quarter. If they have a ring or collar between the bowl and base this is a sure indication of a nineteenth-century date. Wide bowls and almost direct setting on a heavy thick square-cut plinth are common. These bases are part of the contemporary vogue for classical and neo-classical shapes, and they are often found with cut-shapes supporting boat-shaped or other bowls unlike the bowls of wine-glasses.

Again, there are drinking-glasses with decorated bowls. These fall into two classes:

    1. Those decorated with enamel painting.

    2. Those having engraved bowls.

(1) The enamel painting of the period is highly artistic work and the colours are fine. Authentic pieces should be studied and then the beginner will have little difficulty in picking out others. Fineness and delicacy are qualities he can learn to distinguish in them. The best-known glasses with enamel painting were done by William and Mary Beelby of Newcastle-upon-Tyne. These date from 1760.

Another great artist was Michael Edkins whose style is discernible on coloured and opaque-white ware produced in Bristol.

(2) Engraved glasses won the favour they undoubtedly enjoy, more for their piquant associations than for great artistic merit. This applies especially to Jacobite glasses commemorating those exiled Stuarts, the Old and Young Pretenders, each in turn the "King over the Water" as loyalists used to indicate by toasting "The King" by passing their wine-glasses over a glass or jug of water before drinking.

Long before Jacobite days the pioneer Verzeline, already mentioned, engraved some of his glasses with a diamond-point. In Jacobite times the engraving was done by a wheel. Apart from the famous Jacobite glasses, there is the class of "flowered" engraved pieces with vine designs for wine-glasses and barley and hop designs for ale-glasses. The simplest specimens of these are well within the scope, financial and otherwise, of the beginner. Their quality varies, especially in the merit of the engraving, but even the less-worthy specimens have a pleasing simplicity.

The great vogue for Jacobite glasses is not wholly Scottish; nor is it purely sentimental or historical. To some extent it intrigues as a branch of detective-work. What is the exact meaning of the various emblems found on the glass? How can one assign approximate dates to notable pieces?

For example, these glasses frequently show a Rose (the flower of England admittedly) with one or two buds. Does the Rose stand for the Crown of England and the two buds (say) for Old Pretender James and Young Pretender Charles? Or is the Rose a symbol for the Old Pretender James and the two buds for his two young sons, Bonnie Prince Charlie and Henry, Cardinal York? Controversy rages hotly over such insoluble puzzles as these. If such puzzles could be solved much more precise dating of individual pieces by collating the buds with the Stuart princes' birth-dates could be achieved.

This is only one of many similar puzzles. One group of these glasses—the "Amen" glasses—showing a Royal Crown, a cipher I.R. (meaning Jacobus Rex, in English, King James) and a few verses of the Jacobite Anthem ending with "Amen" has caused great controversy for generations. One view placed their date early, even in the 1720's; another suggests a date after the Battle of Culloden, 1745.

Many glass-collectors find these theories fascinating, and there is quite a literature on the subject for those who are interested.

From the severely practical standpoint of the collector-beginner, good-quality Jacobite glasses are expensive luxuries, even disconcerting to Scotsmen especially keen on them from patriotic association. There are, however, hundreds of other glasses engraved to commemorate public events such as battles of the period, political wars and feuds, ships, regiments, clubs, etc., which are not beyond purchase with limited means. As to "Williamite" glasses, engraved to the "glorious" or "immortal" memory of William of Orange, these require the caution that although their reference is to the year 1690, they are seldom older than 1750. In Ulster the memory of Dutch William has long remained a reality in politics and perhaps the number of these glasses to be found bears some relation to this fact.

11

Old English Glass (2)

YEARS ago I had Chambers in Pump, Court Temple in London. One day a member of the famous glass-making family of Pilkington—whose very name is synonymous with English glass—came from St. Helens to visit me there.

He sat in a chair opposite the window and suddenly exclaimed with interest:

"How magnificent! How perfectly magnificent!"

For a second I thought he had taken leave of his senses. There was nothing to be seen in the ancient court but a dilapidated-looking plane-tree in the soot-encrusted brick wall of the Chambers opposite, much ravaged by the acids of the London atmosphere and our damp climate, and of course the dreary, grey, chill sky, looking like a street pavement, overhead.

"What is magnificent?" I enquired, puzzled.

"The glass in your window."

I stared "at", instead of "out of" my window, still puzzled.

"It wants cleaning badly," I said—and it did.

"But you can see how fine and rare it is."

I looked again with more care.

Yes—the glass was rather different, I thought. Not better than glass in general or the plate glass of the shops outside the Temple in Fleet Street—indeed, rather worse.

I said so. Mr. Pilkington shook his head pityingly—the pity of the expert who "knows" for the raw ignoramus or the swine before whom pearls of great price are cast.

"Your glass is genuine George the Second. You ought to take the greatest care of it. About 1760, I should say."

It flashed across me that he was right. For that date, as I happened to know, was the one when those particular Temple Chambers had been built. What a gulf separated Mr. Pilkington's mind from my own! His mind's eye could see beauty and rarity in age where mine had seen only common window-glass indistinguishable from any other.

Later I had my window carefully cleaned and looked at its glass again, attentively. I carried the memory of its appearance in my head, and with that memory went straight out and looked equally attentively at an ordinary modern glass-window. Then I came back bringing in my head the "look" of the common window-glass. Then I looked again at my own window-glass. It was a blinding revelation. It was as though I had looked with new eyes, like a blind man suddenly given the miracle of sight. The beauty and the high superiority of the old glass in my Temple window were suddenly revealed to me.

Came the war, and much of the beautiful old glass in the bombed Temple perished. . . .

I tell this story for the sake of its moral to amateur collectors. It is the seeing eye as distinct from the unseeing that makes all the difference. As the Psalmist says of the idols of the heathen: "They have eyes and see not." So it is with ordinary folk where old English glass is concerned.

So the beginner should do as I did, as that is the only course for the amateur student of antiques in general and the glass-fancier in particular—to educate the eye. Put poor glass and fine glass side by side and see the unspeakable difference. If you cannot actually do this, carry the picture of the real antique in your memory, then the fake or the reproduction is not likely to deceive you.

There is plenty of fraud and imitation in the market for

old English glass. The unskilled and unwary hunter for bargains should beware of letting his enthusiasm for purchasing outstrip his knowledge and experience. It is desirable for him to memorise certain rules by which to test specimens for their genuineness when he comes across something he is tempted to buy.

The colour test is not final, as we have seen in dealing with Waterford "blue" tint; but too green and too steely colours are danger-signals to the knowledgeable. Besides colour, you should regard design, sharpness of cutting, and so on. There is a special danger in old Bristol and old Nailsea glass, for in no other kinds is it more difficult to distinguish the false from the true. The milky-white surface lends itself particularly well to imitation. False specimens even get into provincial museums.

For old Bristol and old Nailsea the best test is a simple magnifying-glass, which will reveal both the perfection of the old, and the poor roughness of its imitation. Also, the fake is not only rough in texture; it is also light in weight. It may even be of a milk-and-water hue rather than milky, and in very bad specimens, of a greyish tinge. Further than this, old Bristol glass is soft to the touch and has a beautiful smooth body like a babe's. Often you also find in the centre a clear spot devoid of the opaline tint. Subject any piece either of Bristol or Nailsea to most rigorous examination. You will quickly learn to detect common glass not only by appearance but by "feel" and texture.

A popular fallacy is the belief that you can tell fine old glass by its "ring" when flipped with the finger-nail. This is not true. A good ringing-tone, tuneful and lingering, is not a sign of age. Nevertheless, English period glass generally rings well.

Never examine glass in artificial light. Any "find" should be examined at leisure by daylight and put on to white paper next to a genuine glass. If the glass is sold as genuine ask for a written guarantee upon the invoice somewhat as follows:

"We guarantee this article to be genuine old —— glass made and decorated at —— about the year ——. In the event of the purchaser wishing to return it within one week, we will refund in full the amount which he has paid, provided the article is returned undamaged."

This is perfectly fair. It enables you, the buyer, to submit your purchase to an expert for advice. The short time-limit is reasonable, since the seller must protect himself against possible loss of sale to another customer.

Very often the antique-dealer will jib at giving a firm guarantee. He himself may regard the glass article as of doubtful authenticity. In this case there is no question that the dealer should give his customer the opportunity to check the genuineness of the article and let him have it for a short time "on approval" for seven or fourteen days. . . .

"Cut glass" is known and esteemed by everyone, the antique often being especially beautiful. To describe the various types of cutting, however, makes tedious reading and in any case it would be very difficult for the reader to recognise different styles.

In the seventeenth century, when the whole process of English glass-making was revolutionised by putting oxide of lead into glass, making what was and still is called "Flint glass", glass became brilliant in its transparency and greater reflective power. This rendered it especially fit for "cutting". This cutting enhanced its beauty by increasing the number of ways in which the light-rays falling upon the glass object are dispersed—just as with diamonds. This discovery gave English glass its highly deserved pre-eminence.

For beauty of designs in glass-cutting look at some eighteenth-century decanters, sweetmeat-glasses or glass candle- or taper-sticks as well as some Irish and English drinking-glasses. Waterford glass is often very deeply cut, the chief designs being perhaps the hobnail and diamond patterns. Sometimes the angles and spikes are so sharp as to make it dangerous to grasp the pieces too tightly.

Cut-glass decanters are possessions that make a special appeal. People ask when they first were used; their evolution is a rather hazy thing. In some of the pictures of Hogarth you can see the serving-bottle of that day, but about 1740, a shape such as we know seems to have appeared. Some very fine ones, adorned with the enamel painting in which the Beelbys excelled, date from the 1760's. Others were cut all over with shallow facets, slightly concave of the diamond pattern, often with spire-like stoppers similarly facet-cut. Later, about 1770, came a slim form of decanter with a flat stopper. The dazzling brilliance of deep cutting did not begin until about 1790.

The familiar barrel-shape decanter, with either a button or a mushroom stopper, followed. With changes of design and cutting this style lasted a long time. By specialists the development of this fashionable type can be dated approximately in five-year periods down to about 1830.

Cut-glass smelling-bottles of the eighteenth century are also delightful, varied and well worth the attention of "period" glass-lovers as not being too expensive. These bottles sometimes have a gold or silver hinged outer cover. For the collector, price can depend upon the quality of this mount and hall-marking may tell the exact date. (All hall-marked gold was of at least 18-carat until 1796.)

One special type of these lovely scent-bottles should be

honoured though it is a latecomer. In 1819 Ashley Pellatt brought out a way of putting little moulded busts and figures in slight relief, suspended within the fabric of his clear glass fabric of a scent-bottle. The rest of the bottle would be done in deeply-cut faceting which set off the portrait very effectively. Such bottles are very charming, and the beginner should look out for them. If he fails to locate an Ashley Pellatt he is sure to find, reasonably priced, a two-part—a sort of Siamese twins—of a scent-bottle either in clear or coloured glass. It also may have a silver or silver-gilt cover (less likely a gold one) at each end. This double scent-bottle was intended half for an aromatic vinegar and half for one of the then new perfumes. In a rich deep ruby colour with fine undamaged skilfully made mounts this can be a pleasing acquisition.

Or you may find a scent-bottle of Wedgwood jasper, white on the familiar light blue, at a higher price, or yet another in Bristol-blue glass or in the Nailsea manner. Without undue difficulty you might come across one of the white opaque glass type. At first glance you might mistake this for porcelain. There seems to be an inexhaustible variety of these period scent-bottles, many of them chaste, and nearly all of them charming.

Laid out on velvet in a shallow drawer a small collection of them never fails to provide admiration and delight to the beholder. Curiously enough, beautiful as they are, at present they are not especially fashionable with collectors. Therefore they are a specially good subject for the beginner. If they become the rage—and they easily might at any moment—their value would rapidly rise in the market. At the time of writing these words, although these small pieces are esteemed, they are rather a neglected field.

Chandeliers of cut glass, even Waterford ones, and others of the eighteenth century, are too expensive for the beginner, therefore I omit them from consideration. Cruets and candlesticks of period glass are worth attention. Cruets, too, even in Georgian silver stands, are not especially fashionable today for use, and relatively cheap. A lovely one can be picked up for a few pounds. Take care, however, that all the glass pieces are alike and that none has been substituted. Also watch out that none of the glass is chipped and that the silver hall-mark is decipherable, the more plainly the better.

Coming now to freak and curious glasses, beginners are certain to come across many specimens in antique-shops. They make a special appeal to some people: others are not in the least fascinated by them.

In older days bottles of the best ale had names and dates upon them. These bottles are rather ugly and appear deep black in colour. Hold them to the light and a greenish colour is evident. They can be dropped on the ground without breaking, cracking or chipping—a test of their general character which cannot be recommended! Such bottles are historic and rare. There are many miscellaneous objects of this kind to be found made in glass. Others are yards and half-yards of narrow drinking-vessels, boats and neck glasses designed to send their liquid contents anywhere but in the consumer's mouth.

The celebrated diarist John Evelyn records that on February 10th, 1685, King Charles the Second's health was publicly drunk at Bromley in Kent by the High Sheriff of Kent "in a flint glass of a yard long". Such yard-glasses are rarely found to be more than 100 years old today. The older ones were too fragile to survive the centuries. Most of these glasses are believed to have been made at Bristol or Nailsea, but it is unbelievable that they enjoyed any monopoly of manufacture. Nor is it possible to distinguish the Bristol or Nailsea yard-glasses from those made elsewhere.

From the collector's point of view, the length and the appearance of the glass become everything.

The yards and half-yards resemble the old coaching-horn in shape and size. Some are genuine old Cambridge ale-yards used for betting on whether a friend could drink a "yard of ale" at one go or not. Others are trick-glasses which, when emptied or part-emptied, are so made that they expel the rest of the liquid into the drinker's face to his discomfort and the delight of onlookers. Often in the drinker's sudden start of surprise the glass vessel was dropped and either broken or damaged. Therefore old "ale-yards" are rare. If the beginner can find one in good condition, he is fortunate.

Another trick glass is marked "King" one side and "Tinker" the other. Loud-mouthed patriots would be invited to drink one side or the other and out of loyalty they would choose the King instead of the Tinker. Carefully concealed round the glass's rim was a set of small holes through which—when the drinker lifted the glass to his mouth—the liquor seeped, soaking his fine clothes instead of going into his mouth.

Another old drinking-glass has engraved on the bottom a gallows with a hanging corpse and the punning legend, "The Last Drop". A grim type of humour indeed! Of similar sort are those which disclose a repulsive snake or frog at the bottom. The "boot" glasses express the popular hatred of King George the Third's Scottish Prime Minister, Lord Bute. These and other commemorative drinking-glasses are legion.

The beginner may be sure of one thing: that old English glass is a study well worth pursuing. Specimens of the antique have also a utilitarian value, though naturally the really fine pieces are so precious as to deserve being locked away in a cabinet rather than devoted to household use.

It may be conceded that glass is one of those things where in certain cases the modern product may be in a sense "better" than the old, but the latter has its great historical interest in addition to special beauty of its own. The earliest glass will appeal only to the select few since its interest is essentially archaeological. From Stuart to Regency, or even later times, fine glass-ware has had a vast public, and is a source of lasting pleasure and pride to its possessors. No English household is complete without a few specimens of it. She is a strange housewife indeed who does not succumb to its attractions.

12

From Chippendale to Sheraton

DESIRABLE antique English furniture is considered to fall within the periods, Tudor, Jacobean, Restoration, Queen Anne, Early Georgian, Mid-Georgian, Late Georgian and Regency. Roughly speaking, these may be classified as follows:

Period of Oak, 1500-1660 to Restoration.
Period of Walnut, 1660-1720 to George the First.
Period of Mahogany, 1720-70 to George the Third.
Period of Satinwood, 1770-1820 to George the Fourth.

Of course, these periods must not be taken literally. From earliest times until this day, oak has been used for making furniture, nor did walnut furniture cease to be made after 1720. What the classification means is that the dominant, or favourite, wood characterising the period named was as given.

In other respects, too, the period-names must not be deemed to follow hard-and-fast rules or to be mutually exclusive. The expression "Queen Anne" contains also the Dutch influence upon furniture of William and Mary's reign. It must be remembered that new styles of furniture do not instantly appear or previous styles die all at once. In furniture-making there was a process of gradual change affecting first the metropolis and later, the provinces.

Passing over the early periods, for the moment, there was one Golden Age of English furniture, second only to

H

the French. That is the late-Georgian period, roughly between 1765 and 1800 or so when King George the Third was on the throne. Certainly that is the supreme period of English furniture, and it was probably the best throughout the civilised world. It is therefore most instructive for the beginner to study that period first, rather than begin in chronological order with the Tudor period.

With this Golden Age are associated four famous, and exciting, names that everyone has read or heard about. These are: Chippendale, Adams, Hepplewhite and Sheraton; names to conjure with so far as English furniture is concerned. Once, it was thought that these four stood solitary and supreme. For instance, the name of William Vile and his firm Vile and Cobb was utterly unknown until thirty years or so ago. It is now acknowledged that Vile and other formerly unknown makers reached a standard of excellence in furniture equal to Chippendale himself.

The superb mahogany work of Vile first came to light when the treasures of royal collections at Buckingham Palace were investigated. Certain pieces of mahogany attracted delighted attention, and the first impulse was to attribute them to Thomas Chippendale. Consequent investigation of the Lord Chamberlain's accounts between 1760 and 1764 enabled it to be seen that these pieces were the work of Vile, or Vile's firm. It proved that a piece of carved mahogany furniture showing superlative skill in design and craftsmanship could not be safely and certainly presumed to be work by Chippendale alone. After the discovery of Vile, Chippendale could no longer be regarded by himself as supreme in the realm of carved mahogany. In his life-time Chippendale published a book of designs, but though he signed all of them, it is now known that some of the designs were the work of his employees Henry Copland and Matthias Lock. On the credit side, it was also discovered that during the last ten years of his life Chippendale made furniture in satin-wood as well as the mahogany imperishably associated with his name and proved himself a master of inlay-work.

Today the great world at large knows nothing of Vile and regards Chippendale as working only in mahogany. Still, it is not really important for the amateur collector to know biographical details about Thomas Chippendale, Robert Adam or the Adam Brothers, George Hepplewhite or William Sheraton. Indeed, very little is known of these men as individuals. Rather is the collector concerned with the "Chippendale style", the "Adam style", the "Hepplewhite style" and the "Sheraton style"—also what exactly these mean as conventional labels applied to the furniture of each man and his school.

That indeed is what the amateur is anxious to discover quickly and accurately. "How can I learn to distinguish these four celebrated makes in chairs, tables and other pieces?" he asks. He feels sure that there must be an easy answer to such a question as this, and so eagerly asks, expecting his need for clear guidance to be quickly satisfied. Unfortunately there is no easy formula to be learned and then automatically applied. Unlike silver and some French masterpieces in furniture, these great English craftsmen did not sign or even initial their pieces. It is certainly not quite so simple as finding a signature or initials. True, Chippendale, Hepplewhite and Sheraton themselves issued books— the *Director*, the *Guide* and the *Drawing-Book*—which contain copies of their respective designs. Sometimes distinctions between the designs are clearly marked and easily seen, but not always. A neutral phrase "Hepplewhite-Sheraton" has even been suggested for certain pieces.

Books can hardly be dispensed with in learning about furniture, and *Chippendale-Furniture Designs*, by R. W.

Symonds, *Hepplewhite Furniture Designs* and *Sheraton Furniture Designs*, both by Ralph Edwards, will repay study. Excellent as illustrations (especially line-drawings and photographs) are, they do not enable the beginner to dispense with actual inspection of chairs, tables, sideboards, bureaux and the rest. Here the beauty of craftsmanship can be seen, as well as other beauties such as design and proportions. Only experience in inspection enables the expert to tell at a glance which school—Chippendale, Adams, Hepplewhite or Sheraton—an eighteenth-century piece of furniture belongs.

However, there are broad distinctions which can be stated here and which will assist the amateur. For instance, the Adams brothers revived the classical style; this kind of ornamentation and design is heavily represented in practically all their work. This prominent feature sharply and clearly distinguishes their furniture from that of their great contemporaries. Again, Chippendale, broadly speaking, favours heavy carven mahogany while Sheraton's favourite wood appears to be satinwood. Hepplewhite, too, has a lighter style in his designs than Chippendale, rather resembling French work.

There are also distinctive touches. Carved cabriole legs and claw-and-ball feet for instance are prominent characteristics of Chippendale. (Cabriole means a leg curved in form and having a sudden arch outwards at the top.) Sheraton seems especially to run to kidney-shaped tables —often said to be his invention—and to ingenious secret drawers and semi-mechanical contrivances. Again, while Sheraton sideboards are deservedly famous, Chippendale hardly produced any, preferring side- and carving-tables often fitted with marble tops.

The Chippendale school made a great variety of articles such as bureau book-cases, tripod and dining-tables, settees, card-tables, commodes, tester and four-poster bedsteads, firescreens, knife-boxes, tea-caddies. etc. The Adams brothers produced sideboards with taper pedestals, commodes, vase-shaped knife-cabinets, book-cases, girandoles (bracket chandeliers), mirror-frames, tables, etc. Hepplewhite produced winged easy-chairs, finely inlaid tea-caddies and trays, swing mirrors, writing-tables, large cabinets, knife-urns, grandfather-clock cases, tables, etc. Sheraton, as well as his sideboards with convex corners (this distinguishes them from Hepplewhite with concave corners), produced library-steps, "harlequin" tables, chairs, pen-troughs, writing slopes, etc.

Treatises have been written upon the varied articles of household equipment created by these masters of furniture-production and their schools. The subject is vast; here it can only be dealt with by considering one common object as produced by each school. Let us take, for example, the chair.

So far as Chippendale chairs are concerned, attention has already been directed to the especial use of carved cabriole legs and claw-and-ball feet. Where the claw is that of a lion, it is earlier in date than that of an eagle. The splat (i.e. the middle piece of a chair-back) is often most elaborately carved, as in a "ribbon-back" chair, a ladder-back chair, a "superimposed-ellipses" chair, or those in the Chinese taste. The letters "C" and "S" are other frequent designs.

Knees of Chippendale chairs are often decorated with carved scrolls, cabuchons, acanthus leaves and so forth. The top rails of dining-chairs were seldom straight, the line being broken at the ends or in the centre. Chippendale's style was copied by contemporaries such as Edwards, Darley, Ince, Mayhew and others, but all this work is dubbed "Chippendale" quite legitimately.

Many fine chairs not by Chippendale but remarkably similar to his were made early in George the First's time. The truth is that Chippendale was as much an adaptor as a designer, and other makers' influence is often perceptible in his work. Indeed, his earlier chairs having a solid or slightly decorated "splat" (a splat is the central part of a chair's back joining the top rail to the seat) and the cabriole legs (already noticed) were directly inspired from Queen Anne and early George the First times. Chippendale did not invent them.

After his earlier chairs Chippendale went through a further three phases. His second, inspired by Horace Walpole's Gothic craze and not his best, was followed by a Chinese type inspired by Sir William Chambers' coming back from China. (Chambers built the pagoda which still stands in Kew Gardens.) Finally, Chippendale was much influenced—understandably—by the French Louis XV style.

His chair-backs are fine and various indeed. They have been classified as of seven orders:

1. Ordinary splat back
2. Square hoop back
3. Ribboned (i.e. ribbon-like) back
4. Gothic pillar bar or tracery
5. Fret back
6. Ladder back
7. Square back

The quickest way to get to know these is by looking at chairs, but photographs or line drawings are almost as good, because each kind is sharply distinct from its brethren. Chippendale's top rails of chairs are quite as varied as his chair-backs. They may be straight, or a Cupid's bow shape, or a swept whorl, arched, serpentine or triple-arched. His seats are usually square or squarish, slightly tapering towards the back. At times the front rail of the seat may be serpentine or slightly bowed. Here again, illustrations are hardly less revealing to the student than actual inspection of the chairs themselves.

Coming now to the lower parts of the chair, Chippendale made two types of leg: the cabriole and the straight. The straight has numerous variants. Some are slender clustered columns. Other legs have applied fret-work. In rare instances he had pierced legs with fret carving. "Stretchers" —a word used to denote the rails joining the legs of a chair —in Chippendale chairs are found with the straight legs, not with the cabriole. Chippendale's stretchers are usually plain, but sometimes carved or pierced.

The feet of a Chippendale chair show many variations. The claw-and-ball foot—a great favourite of his and of his disciples and imitators—has already been noticed. There are also web, scroll, leaf, paw and dolphin types. The slipper foot speaks of his middle period.

Useful though they are in general, you will find photographs in books not good enough very often for illustrating the feet of a Chippendale chair. Careful drawings are better: these show the different types much more clearly than photographs reproduced in books or magazines generally. To recognise the typical and varied feet it is most desirable to inspect actual Chippendale chairs.

So much for the Chippendale chair. Next apply the method of detailed inspection, set out here, to the various chair parts—back, rail, seat, legs, stretcher and feet—to other Chippendale articles. Methodically study the characteristics of each part of a bed, cabinet or table, book-case, secretaire, sofa and the rest, then you cannot fail in your Chippendale education. The same systematic inspection in detail is equally rewarding with other makers.

Consider next the Adam chair. With the coming of the

Adam brothers into furniture-designing, an entire change took place in the form of the English chair. The Adams were classicists with all the distinctive style that the description denotes. The cabriole leg was not an ideal of theirs: something more severe was required. The austerity of the ancients was applied by them even to the comfort-giving chair. So in place of the curved cabriole we find the square or tapered leg with a spade or block foot, or a round and fluted leg ended in a turned or moulded foot.

Adam's chair-backs are square with a slight arch, round or oval. One form is a "wheel" back with a fluted outer rim or pattern in the centre. The seats of Adam's chairs varied in shape. Some are almost square, tapering somewhat to the back. Others curve outward in front with rounded sides. Others again are oval; almost circles in fact. Compared with the rest of Adam's productions the chairs are not especially famous.

Hepplewhite also departed from the influence of Chippendale, though not entirely. The robustness and heaviness of Chippendale is transformed into a lighter, more elegant fashion in chairs. Both Adam and the French influence contributed to this. Hepplewhite chair-backs show originality. They may be shield-shaped, oval, interlacing hearts, loop, but rarely the square back. The elegance of Hepplewhite legs, symmetrical and graceful, is an especially noticeable feature. Many of his chairs have the Prince of Wales's feathers or the ear of wheat upon the splat. On the whole, Hepplewhite avoided straight lines and went in for curves instead.

Even more than Hepplewhite, Sheraton—that unfortunate, poverty-stricken man—departed from the Chippendale tradition. He did this quite deliberately. For, as he says (though wrongly) of Chippendale's designs in his book, "they are wholly antiquated and laid aside". He admits "their great merit according to the times in which they were executed". Lightness and grace are strongly marked in all Sheraton's work. He did not disdain the use of mahogany, it is true, but by far his favourite was satinwood. He also used tulipwood, rosewood and applewood.

No one could possibly mistake Sheraton for Chippendale. They are poles apart. Both in their several ways are fine chair designers. If Chippendale may be described as masculine in style Sheraton is certainly feminine. It is no accident that women generally prefer Sheraton styles to any other, especially for their bedrooms and boudoirs. In his work the French style predominates and in the larger pieces panels were painted by such famous artists as Angelica Kauffmann, Cipriani and Pergolisi.

In Sheraton chairs the back, as in Hepplewhite, is often shield-shaped, but it is easy to distinguish between the two. The line of the top-rail in Sheraton is broken either by a straight line or panel in the centre. In the chairs of Hepplewhite this line is unbroken. If Sheraton gives a chair a square back it often has "X" rails in place of splats. In the early Sheraton chairs the splats did not come down to the seats. They were supported instead by a cross rail. The backs were usually composed of a number of uprights; there might be four, five or even seven of them. Chair-backs were sometimes in the shape of a lyre, fitted with stout brass wire as the strings of the instrument in the French Empire style.

Stretcher rails were seldom used in Sheraton chairs. Legs are generally square-tapered, sometimes with line inlay; a few earlier pieces have turned legs. The fronts of his chair-legs are often ornamented by strings of the inverted bell-flower or husk. Sometimes acanthus leaves are a feature.

Later Sheraton chairs sometimes had a hollowed (or

121

spoon-shaped) back to fit the body of the user. Sheraton loved inlay. The splats and even the legs of some of his chairs frequently are inlaid with delicate marquetry work. When he used mahogany he realised the beautiful effect given to it by an inlay of lighter-coloured woods. When he ornamented he did not do it for its own sake upon the part alone but as the portions of a preconceived scheme for the whole. It was significant of its French character, that Sheraton's style in France was called "Louis XVI à l'Anglaise".

A good place to study the appearance of Chippendale, Adams, Hepplewhite and Sheraton furniture is at the Victoria and Albert Museum in London, where is a very fine collection. Another centre is the Geffrye Museum, Kingsland Road, London. In these collections there are also fine chairs to which no other label is attached than "late eighteenth century". At that period a great school of disciples had followed in the four great masters' footsteps. Some are so close to the master in fine artistic creation that they can hardly be distinguished from him. For example, it is not easy even for the highly expert to tell the difference between chairs made by Manwaring round about 1766 and those made by Chippendale.

The fact, too, that the four greatest masters each issued his book of designs, caused contemporary cabinet-makers outside London to copy eagerly these exciting productions. Hence "Country Chippendale" and "Irish Chippendale" and so on.

Although it may seem a steep descent, while on the subject of chairs it is a convenient point to deal with the well-known Windsor ones. Upon the merits, writers on the antique differ widely. One school regards Windsor chairs from the lofty heights of the great English and French masters with utter contempt. Another can hardly eulogise too highly about the Windsor chair: "Nothing else in the whole history of English furniture has been made for so long in such quantities and remained a masterpiece." It is further praised as "cheap, resilient, comfortable, elegant and lovely" and "the greatest country contribution to English furniture".

Which of these two extremes is true? Perhaps neither! Windsor chairs deserve praise, but the adjective "elegant" applies rather to Hepplewhite and Sheraton chairs. The truth is that Windsor chairs are right enough for a country cottage or for a kitchen, and of their order they are certainly good.

They belong to the second half of the seventeenth century, having come in with Queen Anne, but there are many modern reproductions to confuse the buyer. They usually have saddle-shaped wooden seats, turned legs, and splat or stick backs (some fan-stick shapes). The earliest are heavyish, mostly with crested backs. The familiar bowback of bentwood appears in the eighteenth century and since then it has been the most common form.

They are as British in style as a bulldog, and the seventeenth- and eighteenth-century examples are as honest and sound in reality as in appearance. The very best specimens are as cheap as the later reproductions and well worthy of the amateur's careful attention.

13

Early English Furniture

BELIEVERS in chronological order may wonder why the earlier styles of English furniture are left to the last. There is a good reason for this. The earlier styles are of more interest to the antiquary than to the practical antique-collector, especially nowadays when houses are so much smaller, and life in flats is frequently the order of the day.

Large antique furniture, even antique of the best seventeenth-century period, is now entirely out of fashion. Much of it, made for the once "stately homes of England", is likely to prove a nuisance to most householders. Take, for example, lovely Georgian large triple bookcases. In the library of a great country or town house (for which they were intended) they are delightfully "right". The present-day limitations of space render them liabilities rather than assets to most people.

Nor is this their sole disadvantage. Often 10 or more feet long and equally high, their cartage proves expensive. Even if the upper part is in sections, the lower part is often solid and may require several men to move it. These disadvantages apply equally in the case of furniture earlier than the seventeenth century: heavy four-poster beds, great tallboys, chests and similar pieces.

Once, within living memory, oak furniture was almost reverenced. Tudor and Stuart specimens (alleged) could be found in every country district and were avidly "picked up" by the credulous. Often the wood was genuinely old, obtained by cottage-demolition, but the workmanship—like the carved-on date—was a mere modern imitation. Genuine Tudor and Jacobean specimens are in fact rare. Their construction is often crude, so that the amateur need not bother himself with it.

Restoration work, when foreign refinements came in, may be worth attention. Oak furniture of this time is still heavy and cumbersome, but a Stuart carven chair with damask seat is a very desirable piece of the period. Walnut, inlay, veneer and lacquer came into use and comfort began to be thought important. The Dutch styles, coming in with William of Orange, were a good influence and accordingly Queen Anne furniture is highly esteemed.

This "Walnut Period" as it may loosely be called, held to the native English tradition of sound construction, which is why so many pieces have reached our day intact. The cabriole leg and the grandfather-clock were "in"; cabinet-work was executed with care and skill. Card-tables, dressing-tables, writing-tables multiplied, so did desks, bureaux and escritoires. Rooms were higher, so tall furniture became fashionable. The knee-hole developed and so did the high-backed chair, sometimes made of cane and beechwood. The cabriole leg remained in favour for fifty years or more. Chairs for comfort's sake followed the shape of the relaxed spine, often with a vase or fiddle-shaped back.

A walnut settee upholstered in needlework with cabriole legs, turned stretchers, narrow seat and high back of the Queen Anne period is an ideal piece in a modern flat where space is limited. Indeed the well-proportioned simple style of this period is in harmony with modern tastes, and its chairs are really comfortable. Undoubtedly Queen Anne designs were a great inspiration to Chippendale and greatly helped to form his distinctive style. If a Queen Anne chair possesses its original chair-covering, whether that be in *petit point* or *gros point* needlework, tapestry or damask, its value is enhanced thereby, for the collecting world eagerly seeks chairs with these original coverings.

To illustrate a practical use of this old-world furniture it may be said that while an oak piece suitable for a country cottage might look horrible in a town sitting-room, dining-room or bedroom, such a fine piece as a carven Commonwealth or Charles the Second chair, with its high back and red damask seat, looks extremely well and lends an air of distinction to the hall of any house or flat. It is well worth searching to fulfil this purpose. Apart from its beauty and use there, if bought reasonably, its monetary value tends to increase with the years, like so many other antiques. Upon entry, the perceptive visitor to the house admires it. Even the imperceptive unconsciously feels its influence.

Even a beginner is unlikely to find himself deceived when purchasing, for the elaborate carving takes too much skill and time for the old-time "faker" to imitate. The modern "faker" has neither the skill nor the inclination to attempt it. Every part of the chair has been worked upon by the hand of its maker for a very long time. The piece speaks eloquently for itself and of its period.

Careful inspection and a little general knowledge of small points can be of great assistance in "dating" a piece of old furniture. An amusing instance of this may be recalled. When Treasurer of Gray's Inn, the late Sir Dunbar Plunket-Barton, K.C., used to be fond of exhibiting a fine old chair to visitors there. He used solemnly to aver that it was the very chair in which the great Queen Elizabeth (the First) sat when she visited the Inn. As the "precious, glorious and immortal Good Queen Bess" is the tutelary saint of the Inn, it was easy to believe that her chair had been piously preserved by generations of benchers, judges and barristers since Tudor times—and that Sir Dunbar was correct. He told his story for years to visitors from all over the world. They listened with awe to the story—until he encountered a Scottish lady-friend of mine.

"But that cannot be correct," suggested this lady.

"It is one of the best-attested traditions of this Inn. Handed down from generation to generation," snapped Sir Dunbar. "I assure you, madam, it is so, and there can be no doubt about it."

"But look at those oak-leaves and oak-apples in the carvings," objected the lady. "That *motif* only came in with Charles the Second. It commemorated the escape of the King hidden in the oak tree after his defeat at the Battle of Worcester:

> *"While down beneath the Roundhead rode,*
> *And hummed a surly hymn."*

She continued:

"Yes—unquestionably that is quite a fine Restoration chair of the reign of Charles the Second. But not Elizabethan, Sir Dunbar, certainly not."

Never again did Sir Dunbar tell his story. From that day the chair was Jacobean, not Elizabethan. The chair in which Queen Elizabeth sat disappeared from his repertoire.

There is a moral in this for the collector, namely, that a little historical background may be useful in correctly identifying antiques!

14

How to Detect Faked Furniture

UNFORTUNATELY, the law of England does nothing to prevent old pieces being imitated and sold as the genuine article. There are difficulties in the way preventing this, of course. There are permissible restorations and repairs. The sole legal remedy—and often a dubious and costly one indeed—is for the aggrieved buyer to sue the seller.

A most profitable crime, perpetrated with impunity, is the fraudulent making and selling of so-called antiques, especially furniture or articles of household equipment. This kind of thing is done both at home and abroad. So prevalent is fraud that many people regard antiques and antique-dealers with suspicion and avoid having anything to do with either. This is going too far. What the collector should do is to make himself familiar with genuine antiques and learn how to detect fraudulent imitations. In many cases this is easy enough, once you have taken a little trouble to acquire knowledge.

There is a golden rule to apply to every antique: look carefully and in detail at every part of the article. Such inspection is a great safeguard and will often compensate for lack of actual knowledge. Another helpful rule is to make the seller back the article he sells by giving a written guarantee, as already advised in buying antique glass.

It must be conceded that in dealing with antiques—or some of them, to be exact—complete protection is not possible. In the fields of china or furniture or pictures, even

A Spode plate, in blue, red and gold, *circa* 1805

A pair of eighteenth-century Worcester wine coolers and
(*centre*) a punch-bowl with silver-and-horn ladle

Eighteenth-century pieces for the tea table. *Left*, a 1710 tea-pot
and (*right*) a tea-pot dated 1780

The tea-pot in the centre is dated *circa* 1770, while that at
right, which matches the plate, was made in 1775

experts of lifelong experience and world-wide repute have been deceived. Such cases are, however, infrequent. Common care and prudence generally are enough safeguard.

Take a tallboy or a chest of drawers. It is not enough to check the outside. The linings of drawers should be specially looked at. Fakes almost always have their linings made of pine or deal. These woods are latecomers, so that "early" (so-called) pieces of furniture in walnut or mahogany which have their drawers lined with pine or deal are undoubtedly "fakes". The corners should be examined from the point of view of skilled or bad work. In old oak pieces, the joining of the drawer-frames should be quizzed. Old oak pegs will be found in genuine pieces. Machine-made screws, in place of them, should lead to rejection.

While pieces in all kinds of wood may be faked, the most frequently faked wood is oak. This is easy to understand. Demolition of old buildings supplies plenty of genuine old oak, often 200 or 300 years old, from beams, panelling and other woodwork. This ancient wood has the patina of age. It can be transformed or transposed into so-called "Tudor" or "Stuart" work.

For these—and other—reasons, old oak furniture has lost much of its old-time popularity. However, there is still a good market for small, authentic pieces. Replicas and reproductions, in time taking on the patina of age, if they are not actually constructed in modern days of the old oak, remain a real danger to the prospective buyer.

In such cases, the marks of time and wear may be genuinely present. Time and skill, perhaps almost equalling that of ancient craftsmen, have been spent upon their making. The price charged is high; the superficial appearance all that can be desired. The dealer may be discreetly non-committal, while drawing attention to these apparent "points". They can be easily foisted on to the unsuspecting amateur unless he is ultra-cautious. One should regard with doubt and suspicion all very black oak and all so-called very early oak with carving in the Gothic style. Genuine pieces of this sort are very rare indeed.

Do not be misled by worm-holes. These can be imitated. Test them in this way. Take a pin or a quill tooth-pick or a stick of orangewood, moisten it with gum and insert it into the worm-hole. Sawdust, or rather powder, will adhere to the prod. The colour of that will show you instantly whether the wood be new or old.

By the use of a pin, too, you may also detect modern lacquer on an old piece. If you find that the pin easily pierces the lacquer, then it is *new* lacquer. Another useful way of detecting modernity in lacquer is to rub the lacquer with the edge of a milled coin (such as a half-crown) enclosed in one fold of a white handkerchief. If the handkerchief be marked with the paint of the lacquered ground, then the piece is not old.

Faked painted furniture is fairly common. A glass should be used on the paint. If the painting is level all over, it is new. In the genuine, it will be found sunk in places where the wood is soft. Again, as to veneers: under the magnifying glass, modern veneer is perfectly flat while old veneer is uneven.

Experts in furniture have the advantage of long experience over the amateur. Nor is this all. If they are deeply read, as they often are, they may have a knowledge of old tools in cabinet-making and find definite marks of their use on the questioned piece. They may even use X-rays in the case of expensive pieces to detect what otherwise could not be seen without destruction of the piece. Even for the expert there is no absolute way to be sure of 100 per cent. authenticity in the most difficult cases. Still less is there any easy road for the amateur and the beginner. Luckily the vast majority of cases present no undue difficulty for that beginner resolved to use his eyes, apply his knowledge, and exercise patience before he ventures upon purchase.

If you cannot feel certain or reasonably so if a thing is genuine, offer a price according to its value to yourself. And never mourn for, or hold an inquest upon, a piece which you have failed to buy for sound reasons. There will be future opportunities. Console yourself with the sensible reflection that there are more—and probably better—antiques than the one that escaped you. Who knows but that you would have been caught, and found you had bought just another fake?

15

Trifles and Curiosities

Now let us consider a favoured field, what I term those trifles and curiosities often called bric-à-brac—the small decorative antiques—readily available to the amateur. They have many advantages besides their accessibility. They are not costly, and sometimes may be picked up for a bargain price. In some cases specialists ignore them. Having been produced in quantity in past ages, such pieces are not rare, as are the great, important pieces in other fields. In addition, they are often "out of fashion". To the ordinary person, taking no interest in workmanship, design or history, they may seem repellent at the first superficial glance. All these considerations make them worthy of the amateur's attention.

Once again the beginner may not want to collect in quantity. Neither may he care for the ordinary commonplace specimen of the kind frequently seen in antique-shops. Yet he may be proud and pleased to possess one exceptionally fine piece of its kind, or even one or two fine pieces of one sort, rather than one or two specimens of various sorts.

There is abundance of choice. Let us look at some of them.

Take old Georgian or even Victorian card-cases. They are genuinely out of date. The antique-dealer does not find an avid demand for them, but almost invariably comes into possession of a number of them. They are made in every sort of material. Dealers in general dislike them, for they are invariably too narrow to take cigarettes and remain shunned and relatively unsaleable. Who "leaves cards" today?

One delightful kind is made with mother-of-pearl, glued to entirely hidden cores of boxwood, and lined with red velvet. Card-cases were fashionable from 1830 for about fifty years. In silver, tortoiseshell, ivory or mother-of-pearl, you may pick up lovely pieces for a pound or less. In parquetry patterns they can have fragments of shell so closely and neatly arranged that 700 or more are necessary to cover the slender little case. Put in a cabinet, or left negligently on a table, a shining scintillating card-case can be an attractive—and inexpensive—addition to the home's ornaments.

For my part I possess only one card-case. It is of ivory, and has the most exquisite inlaid decoration done in metal and nacre of human figures, birds and insects. Needless to say, it is Oriental, but it is difficult to be sure whether it is Chinese or Japanese. It is a piece about which any beholder exclaims: "How perfectly lovely! I have never seen anything before like that."

Then there is the fan with sticks of mother-of-pearl or ivory. Few things are more exquisite than a Charles Condor fan. Lots of other fans are lovely. Equally pleasant and perhaps more useful will be a little tea-caddy of the late eighteenth or early nineteenth century. If this is made all in white pearl of matching quality and with pearl veneer on its lid this is quite likely to be 1840 or earlier.

Or there are fine work- or writing-boxes in brass and mahogany. One of these at least is well worth having, but the amateur should not buy the first one that appeals to him. Study a great number first and then, with educated eye, choose the one in fine condition that appeals most and is a reasonably good bargain.

Gorgeous little pieces in the shape of scent-bottles will

surprise the vigilant amateur by their variety and beauty. They may be in gold or silver and glass; in agate, pottery, porcelain. In each of these materials they have great variety. For instance, the glass may be cut or clear; coloured in ruby, green or amber, opaline or Bristol-blue. Or may be opaque of the kind known as "enamel glass"; or a splotched and swirling coloured specimen characteristic of Nailsea. If porcelain, then it could be Chelsea or Dresden. You will find that most antique scent-bottles date from the second half of the eighteenth century onwards. Many (especially those in china) stand erect and are beautifully elaborate. One brilliant glass sort, done by the famous Ashley Pellatt, may have a little moulded bust or figure in slight relief within the fabric of the glass, such as, for example, a cameo of George the Fourth.

The late Queen Mary had a wonderful collection of antique scent-bottles. To see this royal collection was an education in itself. If you do not want to collect these small treasures in quantity, you may recognise that one or two on a lady's toilet-table or upon a bathroom-shelf add distinction wherever they are placed.

Bird-prints and flower-prints inspire many collectors to enthusiasm. By renowned botanical artists like Pierre-Joseph Redoute some of them are very lovely. As pictures go, many of these very decorative pieces are cheap. Though made for reference, rather than for aesthetic reasons, they are beautiful as well as accurate. The nonsense-verse writer, Edward Lear, was a most sensitive artist in drawing birds, and from every point of view anything by him is well worth acquisition. In looking at work by the unknown you should regard "living quality" as well as beauty. If the flowers or birds seem alive, that is the acid test of merit.

Silhouettes are less popular for collecting than they deserve to be. To educate yourself in a moment upon the

134

worth of these, you have only to look carefully at what is called a "silhouette conversation-piece" by any of the acknowledged masters of silhouette portraiture. Such masters as Francis Torond or William Wellings or John Miers or Rosenberg, Paskin or Godfrey should be studied.

The "conversation-pieces" are vivid likenesses set in highly attractive story-telling scenes, in which the characters are often seated at table. Note the exquisite, elaborate, and fine detail of every single thing in the picture— the hats or bonnets, the flowers, the garments, the chairs. The "diaphanous delicacy" of the Miers style is worthy of particular note.

Contrast this high order of work with ordinary horrors —called in the jargon of their time "scissorgraphs" or "papyrotomic art". They were before Etienne de Silhouette, France's Finance Minister in 1759 (through his "cuts" in budgets and his love of these "cut" profiles) lent his name to the cult. Preceding the photograph as they did, these silhouettes were chiefly intended to be accurate likenesses, which many of them are. That aspect does not trouble the modern collector, concerned chiefly with their high decorative value.

It is not surprising that many of the best silhouette-portraitists signed and dated their work. Where there is no such indication, the merit or otherwise of the work is still obvious. There is all the difference in the world between the smudged home-made "cut" and a fine portrait in silhouette.

Frames are important to silhouette-buyers. The typical contemporary frame—which is the needed one—is generally of black papiermâché with an oval rim of brass matched by an acorn and ring to hang the picture up. You may also find bird's-eye-maple, or pearwood, frames with deeply mitred corners, but as a rule these are not earlier than

Queen Victoria. Before the black frames came into fashion very often the silhouette was framed like a miniature in an oval mount of gilt metal with perhaps a border of paste or pearls.

When the silhouette began, it was done by hand, and the freehand liveliness of the result was of great merit. Even in the 1770's commercial considerations led to the invention of machines for making mechanical copies, yet it was another fifty years before the art degenerated into a mere mechanical operation and then—as always—came colour. Miniature silhouettes, too, were often done in memorial rings and can be found today.

A silhouette in its appropriate contemporary frame— especially a "conversation-piece"—is a striking decoration upon the wall of a television-room, drawing-room or living-room. It is certainly one of the smaller antiques most worth cherishing.

Now compendiums. These are the old coffers or caskets or ladies' companions, made to contain "necessaries" of various kinds, an equipment for the toilet or tea-making or needlework or writing or games like chess, cards, draughts and dominoes. Essentially they consist of a wooden box such as rosewood or satinwood, often ornamented and inlaid outside, while inside it is divided into drawers and compartments intended to hold numerous articles. They were once the delight of girls and young women, but the admiration their ingenuity and workmanship arouse today is insufficient to bring them back into usage.

They are often most beautifully and precisely made, and very much to their purpose. They illustrate fully the passion for elegance, neatness and order of their day amongst "elegant females".

Alas, their day is not our day; and whether they be toilet-boxes or writing-desks, however fine and elaborate, they are not much wanted. Like musical-boxes, of which the late A. J. A. Symons at Finchinfield once had a houseful when I visited his home many years ago, "compendiums" are entirely unfashionable. They survive chiefly because the destruction of such beautiful workmanship goes against the grain of those who possess them. By the way, musical-boxes are coming into fashion again for collectors, and a recent book has been devoted to the subject.

Collectors of compendiums are few. Though low, prices are based rather upon their appearance than demand. Unlike some other unfashionable antiques, they are not likely to return to favour. Their place perhaps is rather for the museum than the private collector's home, but if a beginner "fell" for a beautiful specimen going cheap I should not blame him or her. I certainly cannot recommend them as a "line" to spend money and time upon and collect in anything more than—perhaps—a single specimen.

Glass-collecting is certainly no trifle—far from it, but there is one side-line of it we might consider here. I allude, of course, to coloured glass curios usually called Nailsea glass. You will find a wide range of subjects to choose from in this category. There are glass walking-sticks with spirals of colour inside them. There are reflecting witch-balls, glass rolling-pins, bells, hunting-horns, tobacco-pipes, flasks, mottled, quilled or striped, trick-glasses and many others. As Lord Bacon said, "These be toys"—and some are absurdities! Nevertheless they do not lack devotees and fascinate quite a large number of people.

If this kind of thing appeals to you, there are plenty of these objects to be found. Moderns are apt to find them colourful, gay and exciting even when not interested in antiques in general, or glass in particular.

Dolls and doll's-houses were much more collected in Queen Victoria's day—when there was great enthusiasm for them—than they are today. Children of course still love them. In my own nursery I recall with astonishment a vast doll's house extending from floor to ceiling, divided into rooms, and containing the most complete equipment in miniature for every possible room, including the kitchen, pantry and scullery. You could hardly think of a single article in any house—even to chamber-pots—that was absent from that doll's-house. It was a miracle of ingenuity.

Our nursery-governess kept the house locked except on Sundays, birthdays and when visitors called. It was to be looked at and admired. You might only "play with it" on very special occasions and under the very strictest surveillance. For it was a costly miracle indeed.

Being a boy, I regarded dolls and that kind of thing as untouchable and only "fit for girls", nevertheless I was awed and fascinated by that doll's-house and longed to commit burglary upon it. I never stole any of those enthralling little possessions, much as I longed to. . . . Today I tend to regard such things with a frigid indifference, remarkable though I know them to be. You may be different. Dolls or doll's-houses or both may delight you. If they do to the point of collecting them, you can flatter yourself that you have a taste of your own. Few people today own a collection of doll's-houses.

Japanned ware of all kinds is much easier to amass. A resolute searcher for it can acquire, quite inexpensively, a small collection from a large range of pieces both useful and good-looking. There are urns in red and gold, yellow candlesticks, tea-caddies, tea-kettles and water-holders, plate-warmers, pierced baskets for cakes or fruits, wall-sconces and dozens of other items. Colours are also numerous. The decorative appeal of this ware is considerable. It goes back to the seventeenth century, but was poor stuff to begin with. When Allgood founded the Pontypool Japan

Works about 1750 he managed to marry Oriental lacquer designs to a durability that won quick recognition. He led; others followed.

Japanned trays—picture-trays as they are nowadays generally called—are deservedly extolled for variety of design and treatment. Some of them have lovely reproductions of famous pictures. On the back of the tray you may often find the maker's name, and if he is an important and esteemed maker like Jennens and Bettridge, Frederick Walton, Alderman and Illidge, Shoolbred, Loveridge or Perry, so much the better. There are "reproductions", of course. The quality of the painting on the tray may not deceive the eye. If it should, rub a finger over the tray's texture, and if there are surface-undulations you can be sure the tray is not of the best period.

When one is on the subject of these small decorative antiques it is difficult to know where to stop, so impossible does it seem to exhaust the subject or to cater for every possible taste. Take Victorian jewellery alone and consider the vastness of that subject. One can only make suggestions of pleasant by-ways in antique-hunting that the amateur may like to explore, for personal exploration is absolutely necessary.

What of figure comfit-holders? Or what of antique figurines in general? Chelsea, Derby and Bow, Coalport, Minton and Rockingham amongst others made these and most of them are exquisite indeed. (I do not speak of the continental makes such as Sèvres, Dresden or Meissen, for these are a special study in themselves and for the advanced collector rather than the amateur beginner.) What, again, of antique receptacles in pottery and china for flowers and bulbs? And what of antique wall and other plaques and plates now being collected so avidly today by all sorts and conditions of men and women?

139

Again, what of samplers, embroidery, lace, and other needlework? What of fine old watches and clocks, including the ever-popular grandfather-clock? To come down to almost the smallest object, have you ever admired a gold thimble ornamented with turquoises or pearls or small rubies?

Spare some time and attention for all such things, if only to make up your mind that you do not wish to collect any of them. You may find some "line" which does make a special appeal to you, or want to acquire at least a specimen or two for your home.

Remember again there is all the difference in the world between reading about an object and seeing or touching the same object. The idea of collecting (say) silhouettes may seem utterly foreign to you and your nature—"those black funereal things", as one scornful beginner, now an enthusiastic collector, began by calling them. Wait until you have looked at a fine conversation-piece. Its beauty may cause you to revise your first opinion of: "Not for me."

All this should be done before you make up your mind in what line you desire to specialise. For specialise you eventually must, and will. While one may have a good general knowledge of antiques in general, the field is too vast for anyone, however encyclopaedic his brain, to master within the confines of a single life-time. One corner of the whole field may be assimilated. However, you can hardly expect an expert to be so in more than one or two branches. He may still have a good general knowledge of the remainder.

After what you have read here, you will not make the mistake of despising or neglecting the small and lesser objects generally dismissed as bric-à-brac. Nor will you, I hope, cherish old stuff merely because it is old, as archaeologists quite rightly do for their own particular purpose. You are a collector collecting for pleasure, profit, and self-expression. Since this is so, it behoves you to survey the whole field without narrowing your choice until you have decided upon your true line or lines.

16

Objets d'Art

WHEN is a non-antique an antique? And when—if ever—
does a trifle or a curiosity become something else? Something to be dignified by the title of *"objet d'art"* or *"object
de vertu"*?

The contemptuous outsider and non-collector may be
tempted to brush these questions scornfully aside, exclaim-
ing: "Oh, they are all trivialities, mere bric-à-brac." An
objet d'art is much more than a trifle or a curiosity. For
example, a lovely miniature painted by such masters as
Hilliard, Cosway or Englehart, worth four figures in pound
sterling, or even one by a second-rank miniature-painter
like Ozias Humphreys, can hardly be rated a mere trifle
or curiosity. In the very fullest sense of the phrase, it is
certainly an *objet d'art*—and great art at that.

Also because of the periods when these miniaturists lived
and worked, their works are certainly antiques. Let us take
another example: a non-antique being classified as antique,
using the word antique not as meaning "old" but what
lawyers call a "term of art"—namely, in a special and
technical sense. In superior antique-shops you may find
objets d'art by that great Russian jeweller Carl Fabergé.
It may be a masterpiece of an animal carved out of a semi-
precious stone or an ivory-backed clock faced in enamel
two-colour gold and diamonds, or a bell-push in enamel
and gold or a breathtaking Easter egg in gold and jewels
made for the Czar of All the Russias to give to some

member of his family. Since Fabergé lived and worked in the lifetime of many of our elders, strictly speaking his work is not antique in the ordinary sense. Yet it rates as an antique, using that word not literally but as a term of art.

It is a fair definition perhaps—though there is no law on the subject and no strict hard-and-fast dividing line. To call some article, which from the precious character of its constituents, workmanship, rarity or from all of these, an *objet d'art* is rightly to be rated higher than the mere trifle or curiosity.

There is a true and sharp distinction between the two classes, even though it is not always drawn in books and articles upon antiques. Show a person contemptuous of "trifles" and "mere bric-à-brac", a masterpiece in gold and precious stones and mention its price. Contempt changes instantly to interest. People do not see such things every day of their ordinary lives. Superior as they may be, or affect to be, their attention is held as it would never be by any small object of little apparent worth.

Few branches of collecting exercise more fascination upon the collector than the hunt for rare, unusual, beautiful and valuable *objets d'art*. This is not a field in which you can "pick up" treasures for "a song". In this respect it again distinguishes itself from the class of trifles and curiosities which can very often be picked up almost anywhere very cheaply. *Objets d'art* are expensive. They appreciate in value and are worth investing in.

What *objets d'art* should one look for with a reasonable expectation of finding them? There are so many that no list can possibly be conclusive. Boxes and containers of all types are one large category. Some, such as snuff-boxes and vinaigrettes, are so important and specialised as to have had detailed treatment already. In addition there are tobacco-boxes, comfit-boxes, bodkin-cases, bon-bon and cachou-boxes, patch-boxes, rouge-boxes, souvenir-cases, toothpick cases and those delightful pieces—the most charming of which may be in agate and gold—known as *étuis* and *necessaires*.

In this last category alone, the field is immense and of infinite variety. (An *étui*, by the way, is a small case designed to hold sewing implements, knives or surgical instruments. It is to be carried in the pocket. A *necessaire* is a similar large case for putting on a table.)

Another category revolves around the *chatelaine*. This is a clasp to be attached generally to the feminine belt from which various small, and it may be useful, objects are attached by a chain or chains. In their day chatelaines were extensively worn by housewives in France and England. To the chatelaines were attached almost countless objects such as keys, seals, watches, nutmeg-graters. The finest were made in gold and jewels, but silver ones are perhaps the most common. Under this heading, since one of them was sometimes attached, may be included the quizzing-glass which was generally in gold. This was used by men as much as women and often suspended from the neck by a black silk ribbon. Some have been turned into magnifying-glasses for modern use in the waistcoat-pocket, elegant and useful possessions they are, especially the elaborate ones of the Regency period.

Callot figures, too, deserve a special word. These are little miniature figures in silver or gold, enamelled or set with jewels, usually of a grotesque or amusing kind. They are called after the French engraver Callot, who lived in the seventeenth century and took special delight in delineating swaggerers, beggars and clowns. Needless to say, Callot himself made none. Most of those extant came from Augsberg and Nuremberg where they often used a baroque pearl to form the body of the figure. Not only these special

A monster glass wine goblet, made in 1710, and two travellers' samplers. Note the knops on stem of the goblet

Silver corkscrews, brandy saucepan, lemon-strainer, wine funnel and tongue scraper, all eighteenth-century

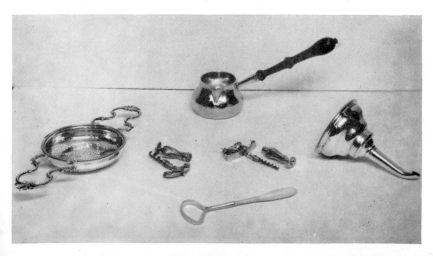

Marble statuette of Cupid

Chelsea vase decorated with work representing the seasons

grotesques, but all figures and small statuettes in whatever medium, may be considered as *objets d'art*. Next to boxes, figurines are probably the largest category of articles to be comprised under the term. Seals in gold or pinchbeck are another frequently collected. So are small bronzes—rather out of fashion at the moment.

Scotsmen incline to an interest in Scottish snuff-mulls. These are containers of natural horns, sometimes twisted at the tapering end. The open aperture has a hinged lid, set frequently with a semi-precious stone or stones, the favourite being the local cairngorm or pale yellow topaz. Sometimes a chain or chains is found attached to which is fastened a small spoon to apply the snuff to one's nose and a hare's foot for wiping the upper lip.

The carnet (note-book), comprising perhaps ivory scribbling-tablets in gold or silver piqué covers, also the hand-cooler (an egg-shaped and egg-sized highly polished semi-precious stone like agate, blue-john or marble made for the purpose expressed by its name) are two other examples of frequently found *objets d'art*.

Unclassifiable small containers holding curious intimately personal implements such as tongue-scrapers, eyebrow-pluckers, toothpicks, and tiny ear-shovels are often in gold and of beautiful workmanship. It is said that on State occasions Queen Elizabeth the First was never without her ruby and diamond ear-pick and never refrained from publicly using it. The Empress Maria Thérèsa had a set of fifty-three gold pieces including tongue-scrapers and ear-picks. Usually of gold, many date from Georgian days.

In the present Queen's collection at Sandringham you may see among other treasures, difficult to classify, a life-like sprig of raspberries, leaves, twigs and stalks made in rhodenite, nephrite (Siberian jade) and gold. This is contained in a flower-vase of rock crystal. Whether this artistic

K   145

creation is by Carl Fabergé I do not know, but it is typical of much of the Russian master's work. Also it illustrates one of many individual objects that the collector may find if he pursues *objets d'art*.

Of a similar rare order is a gold French 40-franc piece or English £5 gold piece which on being pressed in a secret spot opens and discloses a hand-made gold watch. For skill and exact precision of craftsmanship in goldsmith's work, this takes a lot of beating.

Unique or unusual pieces within this field should be steadily sought. Once it is known that you are on this collecting-path, dealers will gladly accept your commission to bring any such piece they may come across to your attention without the slightest obligation upon you to buy.

17

Netsuké and Inro

THE very names of these Japanese pieces, netsuké and inro, are unfamiliar to many people, yet they have probably seen specimens of both without really noticing them.

A netsuké is a small piece of ivory or wood carved into the representation of various objects, frequently human or animal, or both. The word, I believe, means "end attachment". Since Japanese conventional dress had no pockets, it was the fashion to carry objects attached to a cord. At the other end was a netsuké to be pushed through a buttonhole of belt or garment to hold the objects and cord secure.

The necessities carried might be a pipe-case and tobacco-pouch, or a wallet, or flint-and-steel. One of these necessities might be an "inro" or seal-case. The inro was a small box of two or more sections fitted together and either lacquered or carved with delicate pictures of various subjects. Cords were threaded through a cord-holder which could be slid down the cord to hold the inro shut.

From these descriptions, you may be able to exclaim: "Oh, yes, now I know. I have seen some of both. Only I did not know their names." Well, if you have seen them and paid real attention to them, you will know how artistic and beautiful these small objects can be.

The Japanese have always been adepts in miniature art, as have been the Chinese. They lavished inordinate care and great skill upon their artistic netsuké and inro with the result that there were many truly fine specimens made.

At first netsuké were not cherished, and if chipped or worn would be flung away like soiled gloves. In the year 1781 a book called *Soken Kisho* caused them to be taken seriously; it listed fifty great carvers' names with illustrations of their masterpieces. These early pieces were generally unsigned, though they were of ivory and of great beauty. Very soon, however, the custom arose of signing the best pieces, and the great artists achieved high reputation.

The earliest ivories were made in capital cities like Tokyo, Kyoto and Osaka. In Nogoya wood was the usual medium. The great era of the art was in the eighteenth century. After the 1868 revolution European dress started to displace Oriental garments and the need for netsuké and inro declined. The art became commercialised, and poor pieces were turned out on which neither skill nor pains nor time were lavished; these were cheap as well as tawdry.

However, "art will out", and even in the worst periods a few fine pieces were made for export as Europeans began to buy and even to collect. In these modern times a few beautiful pieces are still carved for fascinated buyers, chiefly foreigners.

They were not merely made of ivory or wood, though these are the commonest media. Stag's-horn being hard and cheap, was also used, as was antelope-horn. Jet, coral, tortoiseshell, jade, amber, crystal, porcelain are comparatively rare, but they are all known. Sometimes a combination of substances is used, especially in inro. One family in particular gave their name—Shibayama—to a method of inlaying mother-of-pearl, shell and metals into their ivories which is most lovely and delightful when practised with artistic restraint. Look out for pieces of Shibayama; they are exceptionally beautiful to behold. The skill of the work is quite entrancing. I possess an ivory card-case and a small ivory and silver card-tray of Shibayama work.

When a visitor inspects them at close quarters, the exclamations of pleasure and surprise over the artistry are enthusiastic.

Upon looking at a netsuké, the western observer at once notices the cord-holes and wonders what they are for. Generally but not always they are at the back. One hole may be larger than the other to take the knot of the cord.

The subjects represented are most varied and numerous. It is not to be supposed that anyone's collection, however large, could exhaust them. Over 2,000 netsuké-carvers signed their works and about 500 signed their inro. Okada's book *Netsuké* (1957) gives an account of some 300 artists, and F. W. Jonas's *Netsuké* (1928) has useful illustrations and a long list of carvers' names, and it gives inro makers as well. Some such book as one of these is indispensable to the serious collector of many pieces. Those who only want a few pieces for ornamental use need hardly go into the subject in any great detail.

One peculiarity is that the makers very often go in families. The Koma family had over fifty members, all carvers, giving their signatures; the Kaomi (not to be confused with the former) endured for nineteen generations, though their signed work is uncommon. Of late workers both in netsuké and inro, the greatest is Zeshin, who really is modern, though he ranks with the antique. He has been called "the sublime artist in lacquer". Of his astounding work it has been said: "Nothing was beyond him. Everything he did had refinement and beauty."

How deeply the Japanese carver loved nature is shown by the objects which engaged his skill: as well as human and animal figures, insects, reptiles, fishes, birds, plants and fruits attracted his close attention and imitation. Immortal gods and mythical figures are also carved, so are household or workman's tools and utensils. The subjects of both net-suké and inro are as various as life itself.

Indeed, many English collectors in a small way confine themselves to one subject. For my part I prefer little human statuettes to any other subject, and collect them only in ivory. What "points" do I look for? In desiring to collect the works of a "master", what should anyone look for?

(1) Beauty and quality both as a whole and in detail. One should always examine both netsuké and inro in detail, for this is where skill, or lack of it, shows. Aesthetic quality is of course a matter for individual judgment.

(2) Craftsmanship and skill. Here again look to detail.

(3) Coloration and patina.

(4) Freedom from all breakages and blemishes.

(5) Simplicity and restraint as opposed to over-elaboration.

A word needs to be said on the keeping of these delicate objects. While they can be used as ornaments, it should never be forgotten that they may suffer from sunshine, over-strong heat or undue light. They may be cleaned or polished with a very soft brush but are better hand-polished. Handling does ivories no harm; rather the reverse, I should say. It is for yourself—or any other person handling them—to do it over a carpet or cushion. The non-collector is often a careless person, unaccustomed to handling any valuable or delicate object, and frequently negligent of its safety.

The great rule for beginners in netsuké, inro or both, is to observe a number of masterpieces with circumspection and in detail, noting the perfection of such details as (say) fingers and toes and possibly even the nails. With the images created by his discipline at the back of his subconscious mind, he will instantly detect the poor, cheap, commercial, modern imitation, destitute of the finer skills. Not until he has put himself through this discipline should he venture upon a purchase.

In other words: netsuké and inro collecting is just like other forms of collecting in this respect. Again, there is the golden rule of self-education by familiarising yourself with the best. It is the seeing eye that collectors must cultivate.

18

Wine and Spirit Labels

HOWEVER dull and prosaic the heading of this short chapter may appear, the topic of which it treats is quite the reverse. In fact, the word label is a misnomer. For that suggests a piece of paper, whereas antique wine and spirit labels are never made of paper. A more accurate designation would be plaques. The sobriquet used is the one accorded by convention, and so it had better perhaps be retained here.

This charming and highly decorative little seventeenth-century invention consists generally of a name-plaque hung by a little narrow chain or wire round the neck of a decanter for the purpose of identifying its contents. Most of them are made of silver. A silver plaque engraved or embossed certainly conjures up a very different picture from that of a perhaps dirty and sticky label of paper.

When decanters first came into use, being of plain glass, the ornamented name of a wine or spirit was often inscribed upon the decanter itself. Decanters so inscribed, sometimes in gilt lettering, may still be found today. This practice, of course, had the disadvantage that a permanently inscribed decanter could not conveniently be used for any other liquor. Then cut-glass decanters became fashionable and the old method of inscriptions impracticable. Accordingly the plaque with its chain or wire was invented. It at once became very popular, as the large number of these dainty little things which survive into our time clearly shows. These plaques not only exist in quantity, they also exist in great variety. Indeed, to date no fewer than 500 have been recorded; and the compiler of this list does not pretend that this number is complete. Nor is silver the only material of which they have been made. They are to be found in Sheffield plate, in Battersea and other enamels, in porcelain, mother-of-pearl and one or two other materials, such as enamelled copper which last medium is exceedingly rare.

Those in Sheffield Plate are not easy to find either; and when they are found they may be fakes, for this class has excited the cupidity of forgers. In enamel, modern replicas also exist.

Mother-of-pearl labels are uncommon. Genuine Battersea enamel are highly esteemed. Although silver labels are plentiful they are often of high craftsmanship; little works of art in miniature. Some great English silversmiths have not disdained to make them, and very often the maker's mark is clearly on the back, though very often too the date-indication has never been impressed. Such famous silversmiths as Hester Bateman, Paul Storr, Robert Garrard and Patrick Robertson have marked pieces. Some silver pieces are totally unmarked, though they are genuine enough.

Though Battersea enamels are not the rarest labels, they are the most sought-after. They were only made for a short period, namely between 1753 and 1756; Simon François Revenult is credited with being the artificer of many of them. The founder of the Battersea factory, sad to relate, for he deserved a better fate, went bankrupt, and his effects were sold at auction. Amongst them were listed: "Bottle-Tickets with Chains, for all sorts of Liquors", and they fetched very little.

Some of the more uncommon names to be found on these plaques, names that puzzle collectors, are as follows, with an explanation attached:

Paraketta (*an Andalusian wine*)

Montrachet (*wine from the district of that name*)

Morachee (*a corruption of Montrachet, probably misspelt*)

Cream of the Valley (*a fancy name for gin*)

Nig (*the name gin spelt backwards to deceive servants and others who might be deterred by the strange name from surreptitious swigging; gin being highly popular*)

Mountain (*wine from Malaga*)

Shrub (*a cordial made of fruit-juice and spirit, the spirit generally being rum*).

Wine and spirit labels have been classified into two types: those fitted with chains or wires and those in ring form. Clearly this classification is crude. Many others, according to material, nomenclature and so on, are used. The greatest authority on the subject, Dr. Penzer, divides the designs into as many as twenty classes, beginning with "Narrow Rectangular" and ending with "Miscellaneous".

Some collectors confine their acquisitions to silver: others to enamels. If you collect labels in silver, you may have a large and delightfully varied collection. If you collect in enamel, you cannot expect more than a small, choice collection. Perhaps the majority of collectors go in for both.

There are several advantages in cultivating wine and spirit labels. They take up little space and are very portable. Their prices are never extortionate. You can keep them in a drawer and display them in all their shining beauty merely by opening the drawer. While you are unlikely to make a fortune out of your collection, at least your hoard should pay for its keep. The day may arrive more quickly than one thinks, when these little toys become really scarce—with a corresponding jump in values.

If you want to know all there is at present known about

them from an authoritative source you cannot do better than read *The Book of the Wine-Label*, by N. M. Penzer (1952). This is not a field which is collected to death yet, so there is plenty of scope and opportunity for those who feel fascinated by its undoubted charms.

19

Books and Autographs

ANYONE may, and certainly most people do, even if only semi-literates, collect a number of books. Books have their purely utilitarian side, as we all know from our schooldays. The book-collector is a very different person from the average buyer of books or owner of a personal library, whether large or small. To the book-collector, a book is only secondarily (if at all) an object for the attaining of knowledge or information. He may or may not be a reader. Rather is he a fancier. He may prefer a first edition of *Robinson Crusoe* to all the reprints of classics comprised in Dent's Everyman's Library.

The variety of book-collecting—because as Solomon told us, and things have worsened since his day, "Of the making of many books there is no end"—is almost infinite. So the collector, especially the beginner, perforce must specialise. He may decide to collect certain books for their beautiful and expensive bindings. He may choose them as first editions of famous authors. He may confine himself to finely illustrated books. One could go on and on, for the potentiality of book-collecting is almost limitless.

And how easy it is! There is a bookshop or so in every English town of any size and inside treasures may be picked up, cheaply, too. Even when books are dear they are relatively cheaper than most other articles that attract the acquisitive instinct.

First, let us deal swiftly with antique English book-bindings. This is a rich man's hobby. A good banking-account is certainly needed to form a really representative collection of the most lovely and sumptuous bindings of all periods and places. Even if you limit yourself to fine English book-bindings, you will hardly get together an interesting, attractive, representative and historical collection without spending a lot of money. Neither are modern fine book-bindings cheap. Further, the subject is deeply specialised, so much so as to be esoteric. Therefore I have no hesitation in urging the beginner to leave this field of collecting alone in his early days.

For the rest, everything depends upon your taste. You will of course want to relate your collection to some private pattern of your own. Books may appeal to your intellect, or to your eye for beauty, or to your imagination. Let us take imagination. Certain books are association-books. For instance, if a book once belonged to Thomas Carlyle, has his bookplate and signature in it, and you revere Carlyle (which few do nowadays), you might desire such an association-book.

On the other hand, if books appeal to you from the standpoint of beauty, you may perhaps choose to collect "fore-edge painting" books. This was a technique of treating books dating from the seventeenth century but revived about 1785 by Edwards of Halifax. You take up the book and by slightly fanning out the fore-edge of the massed pages with your finger you find that this fore-edge is decorated with painted views or conversation-pieces skilfully and beautifully done. The edges are often gilded so that the painting remains concealed (and incidentally protected) while the book is closed. Fan out the edges and the picture at once reappears. This is highly ingenious. Often from the literary viewpoint the book is quite negligible, but as a specimen of fine fore-edge work, it will command special esteem and a high price.

Again you may like "presentation-copies" or merely the cheaper, "inscribed copies". Some collect children's books, or press-books such as Aldus Plantin, Baskerville, Strawberry Hill for the sake of fine book production or fine printing. If you are a true bibliophile you will take an interest in points of book-collecting such as, priority of issue, binding variants, misprints, textual changes and other considerations. To some collectors such niceties are a joy also leading to special prices; to others they are a wearisome boredom with which they have no patience.

Autographs are generally regarded as an annexe of bookcollecting, but not all bookshops are interested except when autographs are enshrined upon the front page of a book. Even there the average bookseller regards them as a blemish—unless, to his knowledge, the writer is famous— lowering the book in value. Autograph-collecting, however, calls for special attention. The rage has spread to worshipping "fans" of contemporary celebrities and notorieties, and even to schoolchildren. This phase of the subject needs to be distinguished from serious autograph-collecting, which is genuinely profitable and educational.

The serious collector will frequently avoid contemporary signatures unless fame is likely to endure beyond the subject's life-time. Fame is one thing; mere newspaper-notoriety quite another. Contemporary men of action such as Winston Churchill, Eisenhower, Krushchev and de Gaulle or of men of words such as Somerset Maugham, Bertrand Russell, Sartre and others have a fame likely to outlast their lives, as will the interest and value of their autographs. Leave alone the ephemeral, is a firm rule in serious autograph-collecting.

To the ordinary person an autograph is only a scrawled signature. The genuine collector looks for much more. To him an autograph may signify a signed letter or other document of varying grades of interest or significance. At such documents as these the quest should be aimed. Mere signature-collecting is really not enough—though if a signature were of the most eminent and rare character this would be an exception to the general rule that signatures alone are not worth while. No one in his senses would despise the signature of Shakespeare, Michelangelo, Julius Caesar or William the Conqueror!

Peers, politicians, stage, film and television players, footballers, boxers and similar characters of one's own day should be ruled out. Their value, in process of time, declines to nothing. The serious autograph-collector rightly despises them and so should the beginner. He should concern himself with acquiring original signed manuscripts, of which the epistle or letter is the commonest, and perhaps most important, type. Letters can be most intimate, personal relics of a bygone life and period. An ephemeral letter, written in haste, by Lord Nelson or Charles Dickens, can bring its writer vividly to life. One authentic note from Nelson's own left hand is more touching perhaps than Nicolas's monumental edition of *Nelson's Letters and Despatches.*

At the outset, the aspirant to a fine collection should realise that the very word "autograph" has more meanings than that of a signature. It also may be applied firstly to (1) a writing entirely in the hand of its author as for example, a poem composed and copied out by Wordsworth; (2) a writing not in the hand of its author, but written out by some other person, as, for instance, that same poem by Wordsworth copied out by the essayist Charles Lamb. Now these are entirely different things, but both are of the greatest value and interest. Both are correctly styled "autographs".

Note that in the instances quoted the writing might, or might not be, signed by its writer. It would be excellent if it were. The distinctive handwriting might be such that any expert familiar with Wordsworth or Lamb's hand would unhesitatingly pronounce it genuine. Also, there might be collaboration as to its authenticity.

One of my personal possessions of this kind is a writing by Oscar Wilde of two verses of his celebrated poem *The Sphinx* with corrections by him. Apart from its history—it was given to me by his close friend and biographer, Robert Harborough Sherard, with one of Wilde's letters to him written not from Reading Prison but from Holloway Gaol (his earlier place of incarceration). The writing speaks for itself of the hand that wrote it.

Authenticity of an autograph being established, what next should the prospective buyer look for? Two things: rarity and interest. Of two people equally fascinating or interesting in the eyes of the world, the one whose letters are rarer will command the higher price. Apart from Wilde's rank as an author and his painful personal history, the fact that when the scandal of his trial broke, his friends and acquaintances destroyed in misguided zeal all his letters to them, renders his personal letters rarer than those of contemporary authors of comparable rank and fame. Their value in terms of cash is correspondingly high.

As to interest, the Wilde letter I have alluded to is of high personal interest. In it he reveals that he has sent his friend Sherard—unavailingly—to Paris to see the famous actress Sarah Bernhardt to collect money from her for work done for her by Wilde. The money was needed for his defence. Sherard was a man of high spirit and quick temper, so Wilde teasingly and characteristically urges his friend "not to fight more than six duels a day in my defence". In short, from every standpoint the letter is unique, and therefore a highly desirable item in an autograph collection.

Compare it with another Wilde letter that I own, one of thanks to an unknown Mrs. de la Rue for an invitation to dinner. The tone of the letter is formal and correct and might be written in similar circumstances by anyone of good breeding. But for the signature at the end, the character of the handwriting and letter-head you would not know it to be Oscar Wilde's. Clearly this second letter is a much less desirable acquisition from every point of view.

Any letter is, of course, in ordinary and in legal language, a document. The autograph-world draws a distinction: a letter is a personal communication, a document an impersonal or official communication or record. Generally speaking, though not always, the letter is the more esteemed. The word "holograph" is a rather more dignified way of speaking of an autograph, but there is no difference between these synonyms.

The mere fact that a letter or document may be two or even three hundred years old does not, by itself, make it valuable. Much earlier documents or letters may be. It can be said quite accurately that any such piece of paper having genuine significance for the study of past times, any historic document, possesses at least a potential good price. Early history, whether it be national, international, colonial or personal, is undoubtedly valuable to collectors, and even to a much wider class of readers and writers.

Experience is a great guide in autograph-collecting, but so is wide reading and a good historical background. As a guide to rarity one should regard the following factors: (1) the probable number of letters the writer is likely to have written—which depends on length of life (i.e. the short-lived Keats wrote far fewer letters than the long-lived Wordsworth), the number of his acquaintances and his own writing-habits; (2) whether or not his reputation was acquired in his lifetime so that his acquaintances are more (or less) likely to have cherished and preserved his correspondence; (3) the period in which the writer lived which may render letter-writing rare or common.

A modern M.P. will sign scores of letters daily, but an M.P. of Queen Anne's day rarely indited a letter. Attention needs paying to special events affecting the destruction of letters. For instance, Charles Dickens deliberately had a bonfire of private letters every year in the garden of Gad's Hill, as his son, my old friend Sir Henry Fielding Dickens, gleefully records; and Jane Austen's letters were destroyed at her death by her sister Cassandra.

Quality in any letter also counts. There are dull letter-writers and entertaining ones. To quote an instance of our own day: Bernard Shaw's letters to the actresses Ellen Terry and Mrs. Patrick Campbell made two best sellers. Thomas Hardy, though a great and good author and entertaining enough both in prose and verse, wrote restrained, dreary letters, as did Browning. But Cowper, Horace Walpole, Charles Lamb, Henry James and others always wrote lively, entertaining letters.

The scope of the collector's taste, imagination, sympathy and knowledge lies in appraising the real "value" (as distinct from "price") of an autograph-letter. Veiled references (as when Jane Austen speaks of "her own darling child" or when Mrs. Patrick Campbell says, "I spent the night with Bernard Shaw", for instance), meaning something which is quite different from what is literally said, are clear to the knowledgeable collector.

Forgeries of autographs are common perils of which the beginner should beware. Artificially stained paper and washed-out ink are different from the ageing look of genuine antique papers. Then, too, the constrained, hesitant or shaky look of the pen-strokes may arouse suspicion in any sensitive and experienced collector. Acquaintance or still better direct physical comparison with "originals" is a sure way of detecting a fake. Obtaining an original is not always practicable, but there are books of facsimiles.* It should be remembered that Dickens, Burns, Shelley and Byron have been forged with special skill.

In suspecting a forgery do not lose sight of the fact that a writer's handwriting may not always be the same. Nelson-collectors expect and know that after he lost his right arm in 1797 his writing completely changed, as of course it would. This is an obvious case. George Washington as a young man wrote a prim, legal fist, but in his later life a clear, flowing, different hand. In the case of Dickens's manuscripts there is a great difference between his early writing—as in his first book, *Sketches by Boz*, or even in *Pickwick*—and his last, *Edwin Drood*. The same applies to a famous writer of our own day, Mr. Somerset Maugham. He is the reverse of Dickens, and began by writing with apparent difficulty and ended by writing with apparent ease.

So we reach the sound rule that in obtaining examples for comparison, it is important to have them at about the same period. A Shavian letter when G.B.S. was aged twenty and one when he was ninety-two or more are likely to show differences—yet both may be genuinely written by him.

It should be remembered that, unlike personal letters, legal and official documents generally have a long life. Even documents of the Middle Ages are plentiful and record-offices stuffed with them. English personal letters earlier than the sixteenth century are extremely rare. Being supposed to have merely a personal value and interest, they

* Geigy's *Handbook of Facsimiles of Famous Personages* (1925), for instance.

were not kept after writer and recipient were dead. What would we not give for a single personal letter written by William Shakespeare? The beginner in autograph-collecting had better not trouble himself with medieval handwriting or even with the "Secretary" hand of Queen Elizabeth the First's time, which is difficult, though the personal writing of young Elizabeth, a beautiful Italian hand, may be easily deciphered.

There is rather a dearth of English books, though the American *Autographs: A Key to Collecting* (1946), by Mary A. Benjamin, and *Word-Shadows of the Great* (1930), by Thomas F. Madigan, are useful. The English *Talks about Autographs*, by G. B. Hill (1896), is chatty and informal, but sound enough. However, in purchasing autographs the amateur will find those who deal in them knowledgeable and should always demand a guarantee of authenticity before parting with his money.

20

Association Items in General

WHEN the great Dean Swift expired, a piece of paper containing a lock of hair was found among his possessions. Written on the outside of the paper in the Dean's handwriting were the revealing words: "Only a woman's hair."

Imagine yourself the possessor of that unique souvenir! What do you think others who respect and admire that great genius would give you for it? With what curiosity would those interested in great men, or in literature, gaze upon this Swiftian relic? How many would treasure both the lock of hair and its attendant writing? What sort of price might it not fetch at Christie's or Sotheby's? How much publicity and interest might not the news of its sale create in England, Ireland and America?

Not everyone would care. There are people who have never heard of Jonathan Swift, but they are not Irish people, who still reverence him as a patriot and defender of the poor of his day, quite apart from the merit of his writing. How many English and American visitors to Dublin go to St. Patrick's Cathedral to see where Swift and his Stella lie and also go to see the personal relics kept as national treasures?

This example illustrates what is meant by "association-items"—a branch of antiques well worthy of attention but rarely discussed in books on antiques, possibly because of the vast diversity of the subject.

Association-items in general may be defined as things

having some close connection with famous people or events, deriving permanent interest as well as pecuniary value. They may range widely from furniture to official documents and include almost every kind of personal property. In our definition the word "permanent" is to be noted as well as the word "famous". Brief, temporary and lucky interest is excluded; so is contemporary notoriety as opposed to fame. These safeguards are very necessary.

There are people who distrust this form of collecting. When the love-letters of John Keats were sold at auction, Oscar Wilde wrote a fine sonnet protesting against "the letters that Endymion wrote to one he loved in secret and apart" being bargained over and bid for, so that "small and greedy eyes may glare and gloat". There were many sympathisers with that viewpoint. There are human things to others sacrosanct, if not sacred, from their associations. Nevertheless, Wilde acquired for his own pleasure the writing-table of Thomas Carlyle, understandably priding himself upon this acquisition, and no doubt hoping it would prove a source of inspiration to himself. Perhaps he was not entirely blind to the consideration that one day the desk might be a profitable possession to his family. Or is it that love-letters are one thing and a mere table quite another? Reticence and decency are qualities to be taken into account in collecting, as in other activities. Only certain manifestations of collecting associations can offend the finest susceptibilities or those of ordinary people.

Not long ago, one of the several collections of that great advocate, the late Sir Edward Marshall-Hall, K.C. (with whom I had numerous kindly associations in my youth), was sold by his clerk. It consisted of souvenirs of the various murder-trials in which he had been engaged. Having seen the great man's superb collection of gold boxes, and knowing how finely cultivated his taste in *objets d'art* and jewels was, I was rather shocked. Not at the sale, but because what I personally regarded as a mere heap of miscellaneous rubbish should have been gathered together by Sir Edward at all. That sort of collection might repel and not attract some prospective buyers.

Not many people would desire to own the Tussaud collection in the "Chamber of Horrors". Such objects as the perambulator in which a baby was put to death, or the blood-stained knife "with which the deed was done" can make the mob thrill. They are undoubtedly association-items. In course of time they could become antiques of historical interest, as for example, the dagger with which Charlotte Corday stabbed the French revolutionary leader Marat in his bath.

Such examples serve to show that these are undesirable objects to collect. The murder-trial souvenirs of Marshall-Hall's solicitude made surprisingly little money at their sale, long after his death. Interest in such things quickly wanes. The association-item as defined here, however, tends to increase both in interest and in value with the passing of time. Why? Because that interest is not temporary but permanent and real.

So far as association-items are concerned, it is quite possible to draw clear lines of distinction as to what is desirable to aim at acquiring and what is not. We have shown one, but there are others. As the Victorian satirist says in verse:

> *A clod, a piece of orange-peel*
> *The end of a cigar,*
> *When trod on by a prince's heel—*
> *How beautiful they are!*

The "snob-value" satirised here is of no use to the serious collector. A kitchen-saucepan or garden spade from the home of Charles Dickens at Gad's Hill might find a place at the Dickens Museum in Doughty Street, together with his cigar-case and similar miscellaneous articles actually preserved there. What serious collector would bother with such stuff? On the other hand, one of his famous manuscripts, or a letter in the great author's hand, even his mere signature, all of which are much more intimately connected with him, are a very different matter. So would be one of his pens, a verified lock of his hair, a chair or a picture from his study, or anything of that kind.

The antique association-item, then, must be of some importance, and the closer and more intimately it is associated with the famous person or event concerned, the more sought-after and more valuable is it likely to be. The paramount rule in this type of collection is that it must be authentic. It must also be proved authentic beyond all reasonable doubt.

Let me illustrate. In my own family we proudly cherish a beautiful gold necklace, once the property of Queen Marie-Antoinette, and some pieces of her ivory fan, which broke when her young maid-of-honour Fanny Dillon was rapped with it by the Queen in a moment of rebuke and vexation. Mademoiselle Dillon afterwards became the Countess Bertrand, going to St. Helena with Napoleon and her husband. Later she came to England to act as godmother to her Anglo-Irish relatives and give her names to a girl-child of my mother's family on whom, at the christening, she bestowed the souvenirs. The girl was Fanny Dillon Lott.

Unfortunately, the desirability of attesting the genuineness of such presents was not appreciated in those days. Today, any *grande-dame* handing to her godchild an historic heirloom of this sort would write a letter in her own hand verifying the genuineness of the connection of the articles with the ill-fated French Queen.

No one in my family doubts the authenticity of the necklace, but the evidence is merely of family tradition. Enough, of course, to satisfy the family, but hardly enough to satisfy people outside the family! They would say: "Perhaps it is genuine, perhaps not." Or more politely, "No doubt—but all that is certain to us is that it is a fine gold necklace of the era of Marie-Antoinette. As that alone it will fetch a much lower price."

Now, if that necklace could be *proved*, it would be tremendously valuable on the market. As it is, it is merely valuable.

By contrast, the lock of hair I possess cut from the head of Charles Dickens, cut by his devoted sister-in-law, Georgina Hogarth, is accompanied by a letter authenticating it and signed by her. Without that all-important letter the antique market would, of course, regard that piece of hair as unproven and completely worthless.

Proved authenticity is vital in collecting association-items. Note too that it must be a contemporary or near-contemporary one. It would be quite useless for me to write a certificate swearing to the genuine quality of the Marie-Antoinette necklace.

Even contemporary proof may vary in value. For example, the Countess Bertrand's letter bestowing the necklace as the Queen's upon her godchild would be good. The case would be even stronger if there existed also another letter, this time from the Queen herself and in her handwriting, giving the necklace to her young maid-of-honour.

It is rather surprising to note that in books giving instruction in antique-collecting, there is nothing upon association-items. It seems to be taken for granted that origin renders a thing valuable and that everybody knows it. In such a subject as art it is perfectly true that the whole world is aware that the name of the painter or the sculptor is vital. Probably everyone recognises that such an object as (say) the sword of the great Wellington must be of great interest and value. In books there seems little appreciation of the fact that be-ginners need to be taught the need for and the value of evidence which does authenticate the article concerned.

Fakes in association-items are not unknown. Book-inscriptions and letters calling them authentic are sometimes forged. Therefore such pieces of evidence should be "vetted" by an expert if any appreciable sum of money is to be ex-pended. Where such forgeries exist, they are usually cleverly done by educated and cunning folk. It is not safe to rely upon appearances. I have seen forgeries of Dickens's letters —done in the familiar blue ink on the familiar blue paper, even bearing the embossed Gad's Hill address—which at first sight might deceive any ordinary handwriting-expert.

When association-items are connected with people known but truly famous, the small value placed upon them by the market often renders them very good bargains. A Regency writing-desk that I rather fancied caused me to enquire of the dealer where he had obtained it. He was willing enough to tell me.

"It came from the home of a customer of mine, a Miss Perceval of Ealing, when she died. Nice old lady. Came from quite a good family, I believe. I repaired one of the drawers for her once. She told me it was a family piece."

An innocent remark which rang a bell in me. The desk was a Regency, and the name historic at that period. Perhaps it was too fanciful to connect the desk with one of England's Prime Ministers, the ill-fated Perceval assassinated in the House of Commons by Bellingham?

"There's a bit of paper written by Miss Perceval, but it's of no importance, just saying it was in the family," added the dealer.

170

He drew the paper out of one of the smaller drawers and showed it to me. It ran:

"This desk was the property of my grandfather, the Right Hon. Spencer Perceval, M.P., and has been in the Manor House, Ealing, all my life."

Miss Perceval's signature followed with the date.

"Never heard of him, but I told you she was good family. Anyway, the price is reasonable—twelve ten, that's all."

I bought the desk—an undoubted bargain even thirty years ago. Can anyone doubt today that it has, as people say, "paid for its keep"? Apart from its association-value, which remains to be tested but undoubtedly exists, as a mere Regency desk it is worth several times the price I gave for this handsome piece of furniture.

Maybe you are interested in some subject around which associations cluster? Be it military, naval or literary, scientific, theological, political, sporting or something else: it matters not. What *does* matter is that you will collect most advantageously (as has been shown in other fields) if you follow your bent. Firstly because your interest in your favourite subject will be keener and secondly because you are likely to have more knowledge and appreciation of the associations in that subject than in those to which you personally are indifferent.

It is worth while keeping a sharp look-out for association-items. It is quite remarkable, once your interest is aroused, what treasures you may find in unlikely looking places.

Index